ᴮURREN ᴄOUNTRY

Paul Clements has explored the hills and coastline of Ireland for separate travel books: *Irish Shores: A Journey Round the Rim of Ireland* (1993) and an acclaimed journey into the mountains, *The Height of Nonsense: The Ultimate Irish Road Trip* (2005). A contributing editor to *Insight Guide Ireland* and *Fodor's Ireland*, he has also written and edited two books on the travel writer and historian Jan Morris. A former BBC journalist, he is a Fellow of Green Templeton College, Oxford, and lives in Belfast.

www.paulclementswriting.com

By the same author:

Catch a clear spring evening around half-past nine and you will be enchanted by one of the strangest of all effects that the Burren affords: a delicate, pale pink hue creeping imperceptibly across the rocks, rouging them with sunset. It is a lustrous salmon-tinted glow that settles for a few magical minutes as a long banner of pink on the higher terracing of the hills and sometimes on the limestone plateau. Visitors coming across this spectacle gasp in amazement, holding their breath in wonder. Some people call it 'purple-pink' and it even veers towards lavender. The atmosphere is diffusely illuminated as evening light and the pink coming off the clouds drenches the landscape. Such a wistful moment, although lasting briefly, holds mystery; it is logged in my cerebral files.

Burren Country

**Travels through an
Irish limestone landscape**

PAUL CLEMENTS

The Collins Press

FIRST PUBLISHED IN 2011 BY
The Collins Press
West Link Park
Doughcloyne
Wilton
Cork

British Library Cataloguing in Publication data
Clements, Paul, 1957-
    Burren country: travels through an Irish limestone
    landscape.
    1. Natural history—Ireland--Burren. 2. Landscapes—
    Ireland—Burren. 3. Geology—Ireland—-Burren. 4.
    Burren (Ireland)—Guidebooks.

I. Title
914.1'93'04824-dc22

ISBN-13: 9781848891173

Typesetting by The Collins Press
Typeset in Adobe Garamond 11 pt
Printed in Sweden by ScandBook AB

Cover photographs
Front: Sheshymore limestone pavement; *Back*: The Flaggy Shore
Both © Marty Johnston

Contents

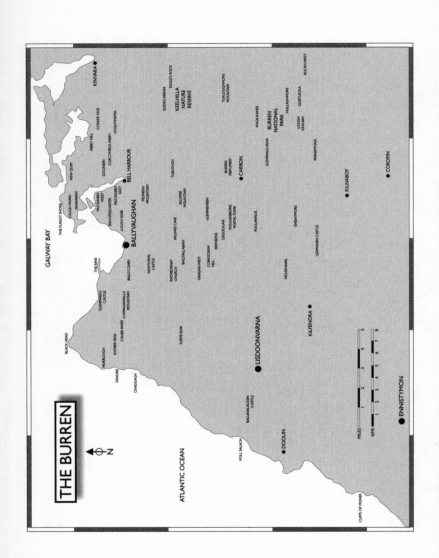

THE BURREN

N

GALWAY BAY

ATLANTIC OCEAN

KINVARA

SLIEVECARRAN
EAGLES ROCK

COOKER PASS
OUGHTMAMA
KEELHILLA
NATURE
RESERVE
TURLOUGHMORE
MOUNTAIN

ABBEY HILL
CORCOMROE ABBEY
ROCKFOREST

NEW QUAY
DOOREEN
KNOCKANS
GORTLECKA
BURREN
NATIONAL
PARK
PARAUGHMORE

LOUGH MURRI
RAHASANE
TURLOUGH
LOUGH
GEALAIN

THE FLAGGY SHORE
FINAVARRA
BELL HARBOUR
BURREN
PERFUMERY
CARRON

PARKNABINNIA
MUCKINISH
EAST
CARRON

MORIEN
MOUNTAIN
SLIEVENAGLASHA
RINAMONA

THE RINE
BISHOPSQUARTER
MUCKINISH
WEST
LOUGH RASK
AILWEE
MOUNTAIN

BALLYVAUGHAN
 AILWEE CAVE
GLENINAGH
SHESHYMORE
KILNABOY

GLENINAGH
CASTLE
NEWTOWN
CASTLE
GLENSLADE
CORROFIN

BLACK HEAD
BALLYCONRY
RATHBORNEY
CHURCH
BALLINALACKAN
POULNABRONE
PORTAL TOMB
POULAWACK

MURROUGH
CAHER RIVER
CARRANWALLA
MOUNTAIN
CORKSCREW
HILL
LISDOOGAN
BERNEENS

FANORE
SLIEVE ELVA
GRAGAN WEST
LEAMANEH CASTLE

CRAGGAGH
LISDOONVARNA

POLL SALACH

BALLINALACKEN
CASTLE
KILFENORA
NOUGHAVAL

DOOLIN

CLIFFS OF MOHER

MILES
KMS

ENNISTYMON

Burren Prayer

Gentians and lady's bedstraw embroider her frock.
Her pockets are full of sloes and juniper berries.

Quaking-grass panicles monitor her heartbeat.
Her reflection blooms like mudwort in a puddle.

Sea lavender and Irish eyebright at Poll Salach,
On Black Head saxifrage and mountain-everlasting.

Our Lady of the Fertile Rocks, protect the Burren.
Protect the Burren, Our Lady of the Fertile Rocks.

Michael Longley, *Collected Poems*

For Felicity and Daniel

Prologue

Epiphany: Caught and Smitten

Once in his life a man ought to concentrate his mind upon the
remembered earth. He ought to give himself up to a particular
landscape in his experience; to look at it from as many angles
as he can, to wonder upon it, to dwell upon it. He ought
to imagine that he touches it with his hands at every season
and listens to the sounds that are made upon it. He ought to
imagine the creatures there and all the faintest motions of the
wind. He ought to recollect the glare of the moon and the
colors of the dawn and dusk.

N. Scott Momaday, *The Way to Rainy Mountain*

It was a grey morning in early summer. I was wet and
windswept, and with an Atlantic gale sweeping around me,
I was getting wetter by the minute. A forlorn and despondent
figure standing by the side of the road, I had been hoping for
a lift from Ballyvaughan on the Black Head road that hugs the
coastline round to Doolin in the northern part of County Clare.

Burren Country

This was one of my earliest acquaintances with the Burren and it was an inauspicious getting-to-know-you encounter. I was halfway through a journey hitchhiking around the coast of Ireland gathering material for a book and had been deposited by a bread delivery driver, coming from Kinvara, at the water memorial in the centre of Ballyvaughan. I walked to the outskirts beyond the pier, passing thatched cottages, several bungalows and a pub. It was just after ten o'clock on a Wednesday morning. I can date precisely the moment: 14 June 1991, a day of heavy rain and coastal fog. I did not then realise but the Black Head road is not a busy one. Apart from local cars and tourists, it does not attract much traffic. As I stood at the side of the road with a barely visible mountain at my back, I thought it a miserable and austere place. It appeared to have a spooky eeriness to it, a brooding feel, inhospitable and soulless, with little to interest the restless hitchhiker.

Slowly, the sea mist began to dissipate. The rain stopped and the clouds started to part. Over my shoulder I looked back on hills where the spreadeagled stepped terracing of Cappanawalla Mountain was gradually revealing itself. As I embraced the stillness, I began to wonder about the different shades and moods of the landscape around me. There were few cars and since no one was willing to pick me up, I had plenty of time to watch the chameleon colours, mostly grey and blue. My time here brought an appreciation of the chiaroscuro, the special interplay of light. I could not pin it down there and then but something within the place arrested my attention and excited my imagination.

After a squally ocean shower spattered my face and rucksack, I watched the rain-polished limestone change colour again. My thumb tried unsuccessfully to attract a passing farmer in a battered Volkswagen but he indicated that he was turning off the road farther along. As I kicked my heels on that damp June morning of long silences, I realised that this was a special place, somewhere I wanted to get to know better. The colours were changing – not abruptly but subtly. It was turning into a soft, still morning. Within thirty minutes the landscape had been transformed. Light and rain, I was discovering, change the whole texture and face of the Burren. The colour, which had been drained from the landscape, had melted from grey murkiness into a brighter grey.

From my asphalt-locked position the mist was slowly clearing and small islands in the distance became visible as I waited patiently for a friendly Ballyvaughanite to pick me up. Alas none came. I was forced to drink in the atmosphere as the rain returned, leaking through my supposedly waterproof coat. I idly wondered how the people living here eked out an existence in a place where the land looks infertile and uncompromising; how they survived the winters, farmed the hard, bare rock, and how it came to be the way it is. There were many unanswered questions but these were for another day. Today's question was how to get a lift to Doolin.

The light show was fascinating but the lack of traffic was a problem. I began to realise light and colour are at their most intense here. The rain stopped again and a few minutes later I was blinking in the sunlight looking far out to sea through binoculars. A pair of herring gulls dipped and cried, and a cormorant swept across, settling on a rock. The sun lit up huge boulders sitting at odd angles deposited in strange locations. After three hours I gave up the attempt to hitchhike the coast road and walked back into town opting for the inland route where I secured a lift within three minutes.

~~~

From the next year I began making regular visits to the Burren, sometimes alone on walking trips, occasionally with family or friends, or sometimes just to listen to the silence. In the succeeding years I have climbed, cycled, examined, wandered, wondered, touched, smelt and considered the landscape from many viewpoints. I did not know it at the time, but on that relatively youthful hitchhiking morning in 1991, where happenstance threw me at the side of the road, I was experiencing a tantalising Burrenesque moment par excellence. The die was cast, the seed was sown and it was the beginning of a beautiful friendship. The moment, or rather the three hours that I stood by the roadside, remained etched in my memory. Through backward glances, that astringent morning has been replayed many times. Looking back on it years later, that encounter was mesmerising. The single most captivating element was the quality of light, and in the years ahead it is this that frequently lured me back as I succumbed to its seductiveness.

Since getting to know the coastline of Ireland through hitchhiking along it, I have also immersed myself in the Irish landscape through climbing its mountains, looking down on the lie of the land and surveying its wider topographical aspect. Now I have wrapped myself in one small part of it, suckling long and hard at the Burren teat.

This book is an attempt to capture some of what has turned out to be a lengthy love affair, unrequited and obsessive, a *grande passion* and an infiltration of dreams in which each year the Burren fire within my head is kindled and rekindled. It is not intended as a guidebook, but more a recording of impressions, a collection of musings, thoughts, contemplations, and an elegy to a place of fragile beauty. This set of discursive essays, or more correctly pen-portraits of specific aspects of the physical and cultural landscape as well as interviews, do not have to be read in chronological order. In them I have tried to convey some of the affection and awe that people have for the place.

Even with twenty years of familiarity, the small thrills of

nature – the croak of a night-time frog, the shadow of a cloud scudding across grey hills, the fitful sunshine lighting up the rocks, an exhilarating glimpse of an Orange-Tip butterfly, a leveret trotting along a road – have never faded. They are imprinted in my mind, burned in my retina. Each visit perpetually yields new pleasures, as well as ensuring re-engagement with the old ones and recharging the inner batteries. The sorcerer's magic has weaved its spell and the Burren has marinated me in its mystery and haunting magnetism.

Lady's smock © Marty Johnston

1

Westing and Arrival

A wind's in the heart of me, a fire's in my heels,
I am tired of brick and stone and rumbling wagon-wheels;
I hunger for the sea's edge, the limit of the land,
Where the wild old Atlantic is shouting on the sand.

John Masefield, 'A Wanderer's Song'

For days, if not weeks, before each visit, I am generally unable to sleep for thinking of the Burren. Frequently it occupies late night and early morning thoughts. The American travel writer William Least Heat-Moon warned in *Blue Highways* about these middle-of-the-night epiphanies:

> Beware thoughts that come in the night. They aren't properly turned, they come in askew, free of sense and restriction, deriving from the most remote of sources.

The Burren also enters my daydreams many times at work – those quiet moments when I slip into a catatonic trance before being rudely awakened by a telephone, the ringing melody of a mobile phone, or the ping of a newly arrived email. Since getting to know the Burren, there has always been an intangible romanticism about its name; partly it has to do with the journey west, towards the sun and the ocean, the space and sweep of western skies, the long horizons, a sense of escape and a trip into another world so different from anywhere else.

Henry David Thoreau said that when he was in need of regeneration he walked towards the west. 'Eastward I go only by force; but westward I go free,' he wrote. Richard Mabey suggests in *Nature Cure* that he thought he saw portents and signs in nature of an inclination towards the west. That was the way the sun moved. He saw 'westing' as a kind of primal instinct.

The Burren is unmistakably apart in the geographical sense from any other place in Ireland or Britain. On each occasion this knowledge alone gives a sensuous thrill of anticipation in making the journey. Like sex, part of the fun lies in the tingle of anticipating it. The stranger may be forgiven for thinking that he or she has strayed off the map into foreign territory and is entering an esoteric land.

My internal compass always tends to the west. After I leave my home in Belfast, large blue motorway signs say 'The West', without specifying exactly what, or where, this symbolic destination is. Part of it seems to be left to the imagination and where your wheels take you. Everyone has a different 'West'. It could be a particular place on a map, somewhere in their heart, or a fanciful, romantic location.

My journey takes me through a variety of landscapes, passing the fertile fields of the Lagan Valley, the apple country of Armagh, the drumlins and speed cameras of Tyrone where it is time for a caffeine pit-stop in the Clogher Valley. The road then skirts around the calm lakes, island-hills and far-famed dreary steeples of Fermanagh beyond which the Belfast Express transmutes into the *Béal Feirste* Express.

As I cross the border my sense of excitement increases. The trees, crows and fields look the same but road signs, post boxes and fingerposts turn a different colour; miles become kilometres, the currency changes from sterling to euro, and the mobile phone bleeps to a new network provider welcoming me to 'Ireland'. The view through the car windscreen encompasses the mountains of Leitrim, the Glencar Valley and long white bungalows standing against the wind on Sligo hillsides before turning due south through Mayo's wide horizons. Low, drystone walls and fields filled with cattle, sheep and horses lifting their heads occasionally, casting a curious glance at the cars rushing past, make up the flat countryside of east Galway. Finally the 'promised land' of Clare looms ahead and journey's end. When I first started going to the Burren, the route went through twenty-seven towns and villages. It is a measure of how Ireland's road system has changed that, in twenty years, sixteen of these towns are now bypassed, liberated from thousands of cars and lorries each day, and returned to pastoral backwaters ironically encircled by roundabouts and fast roads.

Down the years their names and main streets have been milestones on the long journey, echoing the ghosts of my own Clogher Valley past: the Tyrone triptych, Augher, Clogher, Fivemiletown ('where the hills are green and the fields are brown'). Fermanagh's talismanic and musical-sounding road signposts always bring a smile as I pass them and, like the most eye-catching newspaper headlines, are best sung out loud: Clabby, Cooneen and Tempo; Creagh, Monea and Boho. Next come the blink-and-you-miss-them Bally villages south of Sligo: Ballysadare, Ballygawley and Ballynacarrow, before the busy Mayo market towns Charlestown and Claremorris. Charlestown is an example of bypass-itis. In 2007 an €80-million road named after the campaigning journalist and author John Healy was opened, stretching for 18.2km. The road now runs straight as a die through small fields where he worked and played as a child. Healy was a fervent supporter of regeneration in the west of Ireland. When the road was opened his wife told the press that it symbolised to some extent that the 'West' has been saved. She said it would have pleased her husband.

From Claregalway the road turns left and you negotiate or bypass a series of bustling one-horse towns: Clarinbridge (for the oysters), Oranmore (for the bucks of the eponymous song title), Kinvara (for the Galway fishing hookers) until you feel the gravitational pull towards Ballyvaughan (for the gentians) before heading on – if the mood takes you – to Lisdoonvarna (if you are looking for love or simply the craic), ending up in Kilfenora (the home of the céilí).

With the comings and goings of the Celtic tiger, the towns and villages have vibrated with change, but the land, although now dotted with many more houses, is timeless. Some of the countryside is unchanged since the early 1970s when I first started driving the back roads of rural Ireland. Many stretches have special meaning and occasionally cry out for me to stop, inviting me to pull over, adding more time to the journey. The route – much more to me than just places connected by red lines on a map – is part of my own personal history. Often I reflect on journeys I made along it in the 1970s having just started a job as a newspaper journalist. I would head off on solo weekends to music festivals such as the Boys of Ballysadare, take a boat to Aranmore Island off the Donegal coast, pick up hitchhikers, sample the beer in the pubs of Sligo or Galway, meet friends living in the west, or follow the Circuit of Ireland car rally the whole way to Kerry just in time for the Sunday run to Caherciveen.

There is an old saying that the grass is always greener in the past but the light still dances from field to field. Louis MacNeice's 'Sligo and Mayo', one of the five sectional poems from 'The

Closing Album' is as relevant today as when he wrote it in 1939:

> In Sligo the country was soft; there were turkeys
> Gobbling under sycamore trees
> And the shadows of clouds on the mountains moving
> Like browsing cattle at ease.

Every journey has its own fun and dynamic, and is part of the thrill of getting there. In places it is a romantic trip, driving over old stone bridges and bumpy level crossings. High hedges enclose the road for short stretches. One of the most important aspects of the journey is not to be distracted by signs encouraging a detour to Westport or Achill Island, or to feel the urge to look up at Croagh Patrick at close quarters, or be seduced by the high life of Galway city's cosmopolitan cafes.

For the first-time visitor, an eyeful of Burren hills emerges shortly after turning off the busy N18. From a hidden dip in the road leaving Ballinderreen, over the tops of tree clumps, some rounded hills are visible in the distance. On the way in to Kinvara brief glimpses are seen through tall roadside hedges and from a wall on the outskirts of the village the first proper sighting of the grey terracing and network of low-rise hills emerges. They look unprepossessing, even unglamorous. Some people, seeing the area for the first time, find it depressing. They drive through it quickly, saying they found nothing of interest, just a dull sameness. A magpie, flaunting its long straight tail, surveys the scene from the telegraph wires. It too does not seem overly impressed with what it sees. From this distance the emptiness of the hills looks intimidating yet there is a curiosity that also draws you in, teasing and inviting you to see more, to delve deeper into this tight-laced exterior. On a wall, pied wagtails curtsy and bob, welcoming the visitor.

Soon, perhaps around Dooneen or Bell Harbour, you may

become aware of orange or yellow flickers – butterflies dancing across your path out of the hedges, flitting past the car. Cattle with their heads pointed in one direction – west – look serene. There is an air of calmness and otherworldliness. You feel the power of the ancient with a sense of an older landscape, an alien environment, almost a changed planet. The nature writer Gordon D'Arcy describes it as 'a most un-Irish place'. With these subtler symptoms you suddenly realise you have entered a startlingly different kind of country, a different realm of consciousness. You have driven through a curtain into a place with a patina of its own. Sitting on this extreme western rim of Europe is a bestiary of rocks, making up a theme park, a playground for those who love limestone, and a place of international ecological and botanical significance. The road signage emphasises the importance – The Burren: Protected Landscape. Tourists pose for photographs with grey, rain-sodden hills as a backdrop. They are entering a world far removed from the clamour of the twenty-first century and its twin evils of hurry sickness and time famine; a world where guesthouses with large extensions are called Gentian Villa, Orchid House, Fuchsia Heights, Rocky View and Dolmen Lodge.

Having made good your escape, you arrive in Ballyvaughan after a long day's drive. You are now well and truly ensconced in 'The West'. In the length of time it has taken to get here, you could have flown across the Atlantic and be walking the streets of mid-town Manhattan. For the return visitor there is a certainty of welcome with the familiar flowers, roads and fields, the reassuring rocks and boulders, or perhaps a favourite patch of limestone to be revisited. It is like calling on old friends you have not seen for a while.

Standing at the northern apex, Ballyvaughan is a relaxing and contented place, and, for a village of just 250 people, the epicentre of so much. It is now time to unwind and acclimatise to the pace of the Burren. Discard your watch and mobile phone, tune in to the tranquillity of slowness, and indulge yourself in its empty nature.

You are by no means the first to discover it. Many have walked here before. A long sequence of eminent writers and naturalists has drawn scores of parallels with this exotic cultural landscape in which you find yourself. It has been likened to the Steppes of Russia and to the Gobi and Arabian Deserts. Augustus John called it 'an immobilised rough sea'. Thackeray, on his tour of Ireland in 1842, said it was 'desolate'. Mícheál Mac Liammóir described it as 'eerie and uneventful'.

Ireland's most famous literary botanist Robert Lloyd Praeger, who tramped these hills and fields during a long life, wrote in *The Way That I Went*, 'The strangeness of this grey limestone country must be seen to be realised; it is like nothing else in Ireland or in Britain.' The writer and cartographer Tim Robinson characterises it as 'a hundred and fifty square miles of paradoxes'. Comparisons have been drawn with a wilderness and with our nearest neighbour in space – the lunar landscape of the moon. But that scrupulously observant chronicler of this patch of ground Sarah Poyntz says 'the equation of the Burren to a moon-like surface is false, a spur-of-the-moment reaction to a strange and very beautiful landscape'.

Exuberant newspaper and magazine travel articles and coffee table books with decadently rich photographs label their pieces 'Walking on the Moon' or 'A Rock and a Hard Place'. An enormous variety of predictable descriptions have been offered up, creating a specific typecast vocabulary of set phrases. The adjectival barrel has been scraped and rescraped. Take your pick from the following: near-wasteland, desert, untamed land, wilderness, remote land. 'Desert' and 'wilderness' are the two most overused and stereotypical words about the Burren. A check on their meanings in the *Oxford English Dictionary* shows the following:

Desert: a dry, barren, often sand-covered area of land, characteristically desolate, waterless, and without vegetation.
Wilderness: an uncultivated and uninhabited region.

So does our Burren fit this description and answer to these characteristics? In the latter case, it is both cultivated and inhabited (about 1,700 people live within the Barony of the Burren). Because there are farms, outbuildings, animals, and electricity poles, the term wilderness can be ruled out. Desert may come nearer it but (apart from a couple of beaches) it is not sand-covered, the climate (aside from the wind) is rarely scorching or unforgiving and it has water, rainfall and vegetation aplenty, so dry can be ruled out.

That leaves barren and desolate. To narrow down my search for *le mot juste* I flicked through the dictionary pages to these words:

Desolate: solitary, ruined, neglected, barren, dreary, empty, forlorn, wretched, miserable.
Barren: unable to bear young, devoid of vegetation or other signs of life, meagre, unprofitable, dull, unstimulating.

Often dismissed as an inhospitable barren desert and an area of desolation, the Burren, as we shall see, is anything but barren (although there are electronic spell check connections since my computer does not recognise 'Burren' and suggests 'barren' as an alternative).

The Burren always takes the definitive article before its name – it is never Burren. It conjures up remoteness. There is a suggestion of rocks, and emptiness in the two syllables. It has a strange and compelling power, an out-of-the-ordinariness and a mystique attached to it. In a similar way that the American writer Edward Abbey says the appeal of the Pinacate region in the northern Arizona desert 'lies in its total lack of obvious appeal', so too the Burren exudes that same lack of apparent appeal.

Looking at the map, there is a compact feel to it. Its physical limits are squeezed in between Galway Bay to the north, the Atlantic on the west, and to the south and east it roughly follows a line drawn from Doolin, through Kilfenora, Corofin, west of Gort and south of Kinvara. Curiously, its limits at the northern and southern ends are set by two small hills, both appropriately called *An Boirnín*, 'the little rock'. One is in the middle of the Flaggy Shore at 255m high; if you follow with your finger on the map an (almost) straight line south from this point you come to another *An Boirnín*, east of Kilnaboy, this one measuring 247m.

For a couple of weeks on my visits, I generally set up temporary home in a cottage in the townland of Berneens in the heart of the limestone hills. It is idyllic, the sort of place many dream about. The cottage is a simple affair. Formidably lonely and suitably desolate (a mirror of the Burren itself), it is a place of utter isolation that unquestionably meets the dictionary definition of those words. On my first visit I drove past it without noticing it was there. It is not exactly hidden from view but is near a bend and set back from the main road, so you cannot hear any traffic and few living sounds.

From its front door, no other houses are within eyesight. It therefore passes Edward Abbey's peeing test: you can do it outside and no one will see you. The decibel levels are extremely low. The ambient nocturnal sound levels are amongst the lowest anywhere in Europe, on a par with sleeping in Venice where the peacefulness is bewitching because of the absence of traffic. I have stayed in this cottage for many years, observing 'Ortstreue', a term familiar to ornithologists when referring to migrating birds who return to the same location each year and more commonly known as 'place faithfulness'.

Late at night, from the back door, a pale yellow moon is often visible. Gently curving hills surround me on all sides, but no mountain peaks or high summits block distant views. The biggest, overlooking Black Head, is *Dobhach Bhrainin* at 318m. Foreign-seeming and strange, the hills look like a pile of saucers. Although the cottage is my personal short-term home, the 388 square kilometres making up the Barony of the Burren is my grander home. I attune myself to the silence and the absence of noise pollution such as burglar alarms, sirens and mobile phones. On arrival, with boyish enthusiasm, I work out itineraries, spreading the Folding Landscapes map on the kitchen table and fingering it fondly. With a pencil I circle several place names. I like their lyrical sound, find stimulus in the fact that they flex my imagination, and enjoy their taste on my tongue. Whispering aloud the hard consonants brings alive a palimpsest of names: Faunarooska, Ballykinvarga, Cahermachnaghten, Tobereenatemple, Drumbrickaun and Oughtdarra. The plosive, juddering syllables make me think of boulders, granite and rock banging together; townlands and small territories united by history, walls, rocks and hills. The name Burren, *An Boireann*, means 'a big rock'. The poetry of the townlands is evident and I cannot get the names out of my head or work out their correct pronunciation.

On my first morning I wake to a torrent of birdsong. Out-singing all others is a Clare cuckoo rousing me at dawn. For a moment I am suspicious that I have strayed into another world. It is a curiously alien landscape; limestone hills that seem bare, some with jagged points and filled with boulders and walls. The distant cuckoo comes closer. In my back garden it greets me with its call, an acclamation of arrival. It is a transcendental spring morning. Apart from the birdsong, it is a pin-drop silence with a sense of space and light all around me. I feel lucky: wild flowers, limestone hills, friendly bird life, an open blue sky, and sunlight twinkling on the sea.

When the nature writer Mark Cocker moved to the Yare Valley in Norfolk to study crows, he said living there required a 'major aesthetic recalibration to appreciate it'. The Burren is a landscape hued of stone: stone monuments, stone cottages, stone fields, gigantic stone boulders, stone pavement, rocks and endless kilometres of walls. Everything my eye takes in is made of stone, a chaotic mix. It feels like being ejected into another world; it feels, as Praeger noted a hundred years ago, 'like nothing else'. My own recalibration has begun.

Walls and Hills at Keelhilla Nature Reserve © Marty Johnston

2
They all have Outrageous Names

Standing there, gaping at this monstrous and inhuman
spectacle of rock and cloud and sky and space, I feel a
ridiculous greed and possessiveness come over me. I want
to know it all, possess it all . . . embrace the entire scene
intimately, deeply, totally, as a man desires a beautiful woman.
An insane wish? Perhaps not – at least there's something else,
no one human, to dispute possession with me.

Edward Abbey, *Desert Solitaire*

Armed with telescopes and microscopes, tape measures and
cameras, large parties on field trips come from schools and
colleges to study the ground. Earnest students of limestone stroll
around with laminated maps hanging upside down from lanyards
around their necks. They are studying the pavement patterns
and looking at the development of the surfaces. Specifically, they
are interested in gryke density and clint width, and, with intense
concentration, are working out the main gryke directions. They
are also considering the variation of gryke frequency from one
place to another and are looking at aspects of the weathering.

They seem remarkably young to be interested in the lithology of limestone (the science of the nature and composition of stones and rocks). In terms of geological study walks, this must rank as amongst the best anywhere in Ireland, stirring who knows what in their youthful and agile minds. They unpack their foil-wrapped lunches and make notes. When I ask a teenage boy from a Limerick college what he thought of walking over the rocks and stony pavement, he answers: 'Limestone is the new rock 'n' roll'.

Almost a kilometre away a small party of English botanists – some carrying gardeners' pads – falls to their knees as though praying, noses to the ground, like bloodhounds sniffing rare flowers. Magnifying glasses and guidebooks by their side, they discuss a particularly fine-looking specimen of bee orchid. It is a delicate flower with a curiosity value way beyond its size. They could well be looking for, or have discovered, buried treasure or precious jewels: a 24-carat Cartier rockrose along with a host of rubies, emeralds and sapphires that would delight the traders of Hatton Garden in London or the jewellery merchants of Ennis, County Clare. Occasionally they shriek with delight but most times speak in reverential tones. This is, after all, botanical holy ground and they have come to worship and revere in a wild garden home to stones left undisturbed for thousands of years because there was no land to plough around them.

Three bare-kneed women supported by hazel sticks quarter the limestone, stooping over a clump of mountain avens. They are in intimate communion with the ground. Some may even be reduced to tears by their minute encounters with the inner world of flowers. One woman, a well-upholstered sixty-something, calls a co-botanist over to study maidenhair fern sheltering in a damp shadowy cleft. So besotted are they by their treasures that, unseen by them, a hare tiptoes across the clints, reconnoitres the land and gives them a curious stare before darting away at speed. It is May and they are here for their spring love-in with the flora. They have come on a pilgrimage to marvel at two contrasted ecologies, Arctic alpines living strangely together with Mediterranean roommates, cosying up beside each other in a floral super league. Their leader says: 'The ferns stir my emotions and the orchids fire my imagination.'

~~~

The flora of the Burren has been studied to the last stomata. No other area (apart from the Clare Island survey of 1909–1911) has come under the microscope in such fine detail and been cherished by so many passionate enthusiasts of every hue for such a long period of time. The unique personality of each plant – its architecture, its engineering and its anatomy – has intrigued many. Biologically it is the best-documented portion of land in Ireland. They come here for their theses, their diplomas, their treatises and excavations, to test a hypothesis for the fulfilment of their doctorate papers, for pleasure and for quiet contemplation. They come in twos and threes, in delegations and droves. Some come to potter, others to search, find and record, while some lead others showing off their knowledge of the grandiose names of the flowers. Grants and financial help from all manner of funding organisations are awarded to students, botanical heavyweights and biodiversity checklisters to help in their research. Hours, days, weeks and months of patient study are rewarded with a new scientific line of enquiry. Experts on floristics (the study of what grows where) and those interested in phytosociology (the study of plant communities) spend exciting days here.

The ground and the sea around the Burren have been intensely inspected attracting scientists and hunter-gathering amateurs questing for the unusual or their own particular goals in this place of complexity. It has seduced antiquarians, historians and travel writers; enthralled botanists, orchidologists, bryologists, pteridologists, zoologists, mycologists, conchologists, and lichenologists. It has enchanted painters, photographers, film-makers, folklorists, cartographers and geographers; intrigued geologists, palaeontologists, archaeologists and geomorphologists; delighted entomologists, ornithologists, mammalogists and lepidopterists; challenged potholers, speleologists and hydrologists; amused, bemused and charmed a host of walkers, rock-climbers, nature worshippers, plant colour specialists and landscape detectives; enticed a string of lovers, loners and losers, hippies and hedonists, butterfly- and moonbeam-chasers, cloud-appreciaters, stargazers, flower-freaks, goat ecologists, deep sea anglers, oceanographers and marine scientists; beguiled a menagerie of escapers, dreamers, dropouts and downwardly mobile misfits, as well as connoisseurs of ocean views, analyzers of silences, body-boarders, riders of great breakers and thrill-seekers.

For many people, spiritual respite, relaxation and renewal are high on their list of reasons to visit. Others come to gaze at the western skies and seas or simply bask in the sensation of the experience of being here. For these few, it is enough to quaff the salty air and tread the limestone. Anyone with a passion for wildlife, the outdoors and the environment has passed through. Some come just for a holiday – or like me to smell the earth, listen to the silences and watch the dancing light reflect on the pavement.

Another substrata of life is attracted: the musicians, singers, storytellers, drinkers and pub-crawlers mostly holed up in Doolin, but also found in other isolated pockets such as the Flaggy Shore on the Finavarra peninsula. Hidden from view in caravans lurking in corners of fields, they tend their goats, shoot the breeze, and write their lyrics. Look no farther than Clare for traditional music. The county's pubs offer some of the best in

Ireland with musical towns such as Feakle, Kilrush, Ennis, or Milltown Malbay – the annual Haj for musicians. And in the Burren, in Kilfenora, Ballyvaughan, Doolin and New Quay you may be lucky enough to come across a stirring performance of 'Geese in the Box' or 'Shoe the Donkey'.

It is also a place for romantics. The organisers of the renowned Lisdoonvarna matchmaking festival, which attracts hordes of single men and women, holds horseback 'love trails' around the quiet back roads. They feel if love is to be reached, then the Burren stirs the sap and will ignite an amorous spark. At the end of the festival, the two most eligible attendees are named King and Queen of the Burren.

In 2007 a new marketing trick was dreamed up to bring in visitors. Leading names from the international corporate speaker circuit were invited. The Burren Leadership Forum began holding what they labelled 'high-energy' workshops for speakers from the business world. The idea behind the workshops, called 'The Art of Possibility', was to promote the inspirational qualities of the area. The forum was set up by a group of business people who shared a conviction that the landscape would offer an ideal setting for blending serious soul-searching with gentle relaxation.

The Burren is many things to many people. It puzzles, astonishes and excites. It has cast its spell on a wide variety of visitors. Not only did it attract monks, its vivid imagery also fired the imagination of writers, artists, flâneurs and pedestrian adventurer scribblers. The stones have been romanced and versified by a roll-call of poetic fame: Yeats, George Bernard Shaw, John Betjeman, Seamus Heaney and Michael Longley have all trodden here. Long before them, Thackeray and De Latocnaye dipped their travelling pens into it. In the twentieth century a stream of erudite and thoughtful Irish wayfarers and wanderers, ranging from the scholarship of Praeger to the enthusiasm of

Richard Hayward, were awed by it. Hayward called it 'mysterious brooding moonscape country'. The topographical writer Seán Jennett described it as a 'ghostly landscape'.

In the later part of the twentieth century and early twenty-first a galaxy of outdoor English and Scottish writers including Eric Newby, Robin Neillands, Mike Harding, Christopher Somerville, Roger Deakin and Robert Macfarlane passed through, giving it their blessing. The travel writer Simon Calder described the Burren as 'hobbit country' and said there were 'enough holes in the ground for a city of hobbits in a terrain that lends itself to intense scampering'. Few of these fleeting faces and feet ever stayed long enough to penetrate its inner depths and delve deep into those holes. They generally celebrate its flora, sample the oysters, toast the stout and praise the scenery and sunsets before moving quickly on to their next location on the western seaboard.

Countless natural history books and glossy tomes on Ireland have featured the area *en passant*. Authors, radio broadcasters and celebrity television presenters who have an interest in natural history have come in pursuit of adding to their knowledge. Most call it a 'strange, bare' landscape, giving a flavour of the flowers and its geological past. One of the most curious of these titles, *Ireland: The Land and the People* by Donald Cowie, published in 1976, referred to the Atlantic air sweeping across the limestone terraces where 'the peasants have the pride and independence of shepherds'. They were perhaps Ireland's last remaining peasantry.

One walker who has returned for several visits is the Bristol-based landscape artist Richard Long. He has romanced the Burren stones in a different way – through realignment, stone sculpture and photography. One of his most evocative black and white images, *A Circle in Ireland* (1975), features an area near the coast at Doolin with the Cliffs of Moher as a backdrop. Shards of stones are arranged in a circle around a section of limestone pavement which the artist photographed. He regards his photographs as a testament to his presence, representing an image that stands for the whole experience of the walk. Stones are an essential part of Long's life and work. On his walks, he repositions scattered stones laying them in simple geometric configurations in lines, circles or ovoid patterns. Although he may adjust the natural order of wilderness places, perhaps up-ending stones, he never makes major alterations to the landscape.

In my first few days of acclimatising on each visit I like to rock-hop over the pavement, reacquainting myself with some of the precise geological terms applicable to this karst landscape. Karst is a general term for an area formed by weathering of soluble rocks and named after a region of Slovenia. The slabs of pavement and fractures in between them are known as clints and grykes. Clints are the blocks of limestone pavement – some wobbly – which you walk across; grykes are the open crevices or chasms within the clints that many unwittingly trip over. (Praeger had a variation of this description calling them joints and chinks.) Like a puzzle, the clints fit together in an even and sometimes uneven manner.

Since I first came across them many years ago, the words clints and grykes have stuck in my head; two small words that are always useful to drop into casual conversation with friends: 'Doing anything nice at the weekend?' 'Heading to Clare to look at the clints and grykes.' The dry lakes, called turloughs, are grassy hollows often filled with water in the winter which dries up in the summer. The one seen from Cassidy's bar in Carron looks like an oasis in a grey Sahara. It is in a *polje*, an enclosed depression, which is an area in a hollow surrounded by mountains.

The large erratic boulders, carried by glacial action and deposited throughout the landscape, are found in all shapes and sizes. Everything about the Burren is rooted in geology which I think has the best words. Words of resonance: sonorous, rich, hard, and memorable; quixotic words, and words to dabble with. The lingua franca of geology has long intrigued me. As a descriptive science its rich vocabulary cannot be beaten. Two of my favourite, fanciful geological words with which I enjoy tussling are 'kamenitza', a solution pan or shallow pool of limestone, and 'rillenkarren', narrow, sharp-edged solution runnels that form on gently sloping limestone. These runnels, crevasses and hollows are clandestine places.

~~~

When you have mastered the main geological terms relating to the rocks and limestone, the archaeological side – dealing with stones and the remains of buildings – raises its grey and ancient head. On any walk, however short, you come upon singular oddities and strange relics of the past. Littered with ruins of ring forts, churches, castles and abbeys, the Burren is more than just an open-air museum – it is an archaeologically saturated landscape. In nearly all cases their covering has been blown away. They stand open to the sky, exposed to the elements and sometimes home to ravens or crows. The ebb and flow of history has brought with it a land rich in ruins. The past is inescapable. Many different eras and levels of human history surround you on all sides. The tourist authorities market it as 'A walk through time'. I pose questions for myself. Who built these forts? How long have they been here? What purpose did they serve? The Burren confuses and perplexes.

Ruins have always attracted me and there are rich pickings here. There is one special place, Corcomroe Abbey, beyond Bell Harbour, a flat 8-km bike ride from Ballyvaughan. Founded as a Cistercian monastery, it was named *Petra Fertilis*, 'The Fertile Rock'. It lies in a bowl, in the shadow of Abbey Hill on one side, Turlough Hill on the other, and Moneen Mountain to its west.

It is in the valley of Glennamannagh, 'the valley of the monks', a quiet place of sanctity inspiring a mood of reflection. It is easy to see why the monks chose it as a haven of tranquillity. The abbey is well-preserved and for 900 years has added a touch of nobility and grandeur to the countryside. On one visit, a man from the heritage service told me about the high quality floral stone carvings at the eastern end of the church. Legend has it, he said, that the stonemasons who built it around 1205 were killed when they had completed the job to prevent them building a more beautiful church somewhere else.

Rock climbers come to the Burren because it offers some of Ireland's best challenges. I like the grim drollery of the imaginative appellations bestowed by them to their climbs: The Revolution will not be Televised, Mad Mackerel, Preacher-Heckler, Atomic Rooster, Up in Smoke, Moments of Inertia, Tombstone Terror, Hooked on Crack, Peanut Butter Special, Obscene Sardine, Damn the Torpedoes, and Hopeless Acts of Desperation. These are from an area called Ailladie which, for rock climbers, I have always found to be an amusing translation: *Aill an Daill* – 'The Blind Man's Cliff'. Farther along the coast, at the Cliffs of Moher is the headland of *Aill na Searrach*, (affectionately nicknamed Aileen) towering over one of the world's most famous surfing spots.

Inexhaustible kilometres of ancient stone walls, magnificently built, yet with a seemingly higgledy-piggledy, thrown-together appearance, stretch up to cairns at the top of many of the Burren's hills where small knots and piles of stones are assembled. In the 1980s Ballyvaughan used to boast a chic restaurant *Trí na cheile* which translates as 'through-other', an apt description for the jumbled walls. It is estimated that Ireland has approximately 390km of stone field walls – the most of any country in the world; a large proportion of them are found in the Burren.

Threading in all directions, they are the ribs and backbone of the place, an exoskeleton providing support and protection for animals. The stones to build this theme park of walls come in strange, mixed shapes and sizes: round, flat, square, oblong, rectangular. Some protrude out of the earth with sharp edges. Tall, thin, upright ones, like collapsed dominoes, lie drunkenly against each other for support. Some stand like headstones in graveyards. Long rows are stitched together in an orderly way and have a uniformity about them; others splaying at skew-whiff angles look jumbled, wedged haphazardly, balanced miraculously in a disorganised fretwork seemingly serpentining into infinity. Yet they are fundamental components of the landscape and have an element of artistry to them.

I have puzzled over where they start and finish. Who decides where the boundaries are and to whom do they belong? The walls mark out the boundaries of the different areas but because many have collapsed or are obsolete their divisions are not clear. Wall aficionados come to study the patterns. There are several types all with different stone arrangements. These include shelter walls, slab walls (fixed into the grykes with upended limestone flags) tumble walls, single stone walls and double walls. They are sculpted into the contours of the landscape, but most visitors do not appreciate their lightly worn beauty. The walls are a familiar and essential feature of the outdoor life of the place. A monument to craftsmanship from a bygone age, they stand like forgotten relics, yet the spirits of the past still live in their stone legacy.

~~~

The Burren can drown you in statistics. Hundreds of biological, geological and archaeological facts are offered up to first-time visitors stopping them in their tracks. The unexpected hits you

27

round every corner. Guidebook figures inform you matter-of-factly that there are 10 types of willow tree, 23 orchids, 24 different species of dandelion, 25 ferns, 30 species of butterflies, 50 grasses, 70 land snails, 84 recorded examples of wedge-tombs, 254 caves, 270 moths, 450 ring forts (or 500 depending on which book you read) and at least 700 plant species, including trees and ferns, have been documented. Archaeologists have recorded more than 2,000 monuments, three times the national average. The two main types of rock, the Carboniferous limestone and the Clare Shales, were deposited between 320 and 360 million years ago. In the building of Cahercommaun cliff fort, 16,500 cubic metres of stone were used, and there are 36,000 hectares of limestone pavement which equates to ten times more than in Britain. More shrubby cinquefoil grows here than anywhere else in western Europe.

The Burren feels good about itself. It is not averse to gushing promotion of its image. It is a place of startling numbers and factoids that bamboozle you as you try to get your head round them and work out where they all came from and how they ended up here. Although the Burren represents just 1 per cent of the landmass of Ireland, 70 per cent of its native species is found here. Information and figures on an international scale are thrown up about the place and they always astound.

There are enough facts – enough biggest, best, oldest, longest and deepest – to grace a page of the *Guinness Book of World Records*. The biggest turlough in Europe is at Carron (best viewed from the comfort of Cassidy's, a former police barracks and now a pub); the largest (reputedly) free-hanging stalactite in the world, the Great Stalactite at 7m, is found at Pól an Ionáin cave near Doolin; the Polnagollum complex on the eastern side of Slieve Elva is thought to be the longest cave system in western Europe with 16km of mapped passages. It is also believed to be the cave that inspired J. R. R. Tolkien's *The Lord of the*

Rings character Gollum and in 2010 a website was set up to promote the connection; the slow-worm, a small, legless lizard, was first seen here in 1971 and the Burren has the only Irish breeding colony of the creature; the first colony of the only Irish location of the land winkle (*Pomatias elegans*) was discovered on a northwest-facing slope on an isolated peninsula near New Quay in July 1976. Lurking under cushions of vegetation on the exposed edges of limestone slabs and clinging to the sides of the grykes, *P. elegans* thrilled the Irish mollusc world.

There is a veritable landslide of commentary on the Burren. Mountains of reports and papers have been written on a multitude of different aspects of the place – most of it published in the past 150 years. One of the earliest was Frederick Foot's paper on the distribution of plants in the Burren which was read to the Royal Irish Academy (RIA) on 28 April 1862. Published in the Academy's august journal, it stretches to twenty pages. In 1911, according to Praeger on a visit to the Burren, distinguished botanists from the International Phytogeographical Excursion discussed the topic of patches of thin peat directly over the limestone.

Since the early 1990s there has been renewed vigour with more masterly papers added to the ever-growing pile. Many of these clearly are not intended for the general reader. Thumbing through the library in the Burren College of Art at Newtown Castle one wet morning, I came across references to hundreds of articles published in a huge variety of journals covering everything from the flora to caves, and from aspects of biological weathering to fluid inclusion studies combined with rare earth element geochemistry of Burren fluorite veins. Scores of scholarly papers have been published in any number of esoteric journals to satisfy the craving for knowledge, whether for academics or amateur history buffs.

The Proceedings of the RIA contain many articles featuring

scientific studies of the Burren and could form a magisterial book on its own. The Academy, with its admirable motto 'We Will Endeavour', has produced papers on many arcane topics and investigations carried out in the region as well as supporting much new research. In 2003, it published nine scientific papers on experimentally based studies in a single volume called *Understanding the Burren*. Using random selection, I made a note of some of the obscure topics studied:

> – a two-site study, in October 1999 and April 2000, which examined the physico-chemical characteristics and the macro invertebrate communities of the Caher River, the only river that rises in the Burren;
> – a three-year study (1997–1999) looked at sporocarp abundance in plots of *Dryas octopetala* and assessed the relationships among macro fungi, vegetation and soil variables;
> – a year-long survey produced a comparative assessment of the phytoplankton and charophytes of Lough Bunny, a karst lake in the eastern Burren;
> – another paper looked at the issues that concern plant ecologists reviewing ideas that had been used to explain the pattern of grassland and heath communities in Europe and apply them to the special case of the Burren.

Leafing through *Tearmann: Irish journal of agri-environmental research* reveals lengthy articles with titles such as 'Nutrient dynamics of *Sesleria*-dominated grasslands in the Burren National Park', and 'Productivity, grazing pressure and phenology of a limestone grassland'. A flick through some journals throws up intriguing titles: 'Three days among the bats in Clare' (*Zoologist*), 'The spatial distribution of turloughs' (*Irish Geography*), 'The vegetation of solution cups in the limestone of the Burren' (*Journal of Ecology*), 'Genecological differentiation of leaf morphology in *Geranium sanguineum*' (*New Phystologist*), 'My hobby about ferns and its results, Personal reminiscences' (*Proceedings of the Belfast Naturalists' Field Club*) and a raft of other essays in journals ranging from the *Entomologist's Gazette* to the *Carnivorous Plant Newsletter*.

Just when you thought there was nothing left to explore, information (and funding) emerges that sends the scientists off on a new probe – a potentially messy study involving a research team from NUI Galway scrutinising Burren cow dung. The team included a German PhD research fellow funded by the Irish Research Council for Science, Engineering and Technology, and investigated coprophilous fungal spores growing on cattle and sheep. For their work, which was carried out between Cappanawalla Mountain and Black Head, they dug out peat sods which had preserved the spores. Through radiocarbon dating, this led to a clearer picture of the impact of human activity and farming in the Burren over the last 3,500 years.

A large body of published work exists on the ecology of turloughs including their habitats and their biota. A study on the amphibious lifestyles, the sensitivities of the organisms in adapting to depth, temperature or frequency and the pattern of floating as well as possibilities for conservation have intrigued hydrologists. Ecological comparisons of water bodies have been made, with detailed notes on the hemipetra, coleopetra, diptera and other invertebrates in Burren turlough studies. Very little, on the other hand, has been written about the doline lakes south of Mullaghmore. Beetle experts were very excited in the early part of this century when they discovered a rare beetle that lives only in the blue-green algae crust of one of the lakes.

Turloughs throw up some curiosities of nature. In the late 1960s and early 1970s the appearance of strange, white, algal paper, or bleached alga, at a turlough appropriately near the village of Turlough in a valley south of Bell Harbour animated many Burren regulars. The story of this rare sight is recounted by Mary Scannell in the January 1972 edition of the *Irish Naturalists' Journal.* She describes how a visitor from the Liverpool Botanic Society approached the lough on a sunny day in May thinking it was an apparent snowfield:

> The sheeted alga was so thick in some areas as to resemble parchment in texture and colour, in other parts it was of gossamer fineness. Bushes were covered with hammocks of webbed alga, stone walls bore white shawls tasselated where the weight of wet material had pulled away from the dried portion, boulders were draped with bleached shapes as though tablecloths had been laid out to dry and whiten. On traversing the white carpet in the hot midday sun, a dazzling reflection afflicted the eyes making it necessary to shade them from the glare. The German seventeenth-century naturalist I. J. Hartman explained this 'paper' as having fallen from heaven and being of meteoric nature.

Generations of butterfly hunters with their nets and collecting bags have been drawn to the area to spend long days studying the dazzling iridescence of butterflies' wings. The Burren is a butterfly-friendly 'hot-spot'. The aurelians (a fancy named for lepidopterists) come, praying for sunny weather, and are often rewarded. During a five-minute period in early July 2008, at a butterfly site at Termon, they recorded twenty-six individual Dark Green Fritillaries. Scientists like grid references and can pinpoint the exact breeding ground of the Marsh Fritillary covering an area only 280m by 90m. More than thirty different species of butterfly (including twenty-six residents) have been noted in the Burren. Some are more widespread than others and a few are scarce or local. But whatever time of the summer, each species – from the Common Blue to the Brown Hairstreak – is a part of the natural and cultural identity of the landscape.

Twenty-two of Ireland's leading bee specialists descended on the Burren for a weekend Bee Blitz of apitherapy in July 2010. Along the coast at Fanore Beg they identified a new population of the Great Yellow Bumblebee (*Bombus distinguendus*) which is threatened with extinction. Under the auspices of the National Biodiversity Data Centre in Waterford, the apidologists carried out detailed systematic surveys of the area which contains three-quarters of all the species of bumblebee found in Ireland. The Burren is important for bumblebees because it is species-rich and is home to many rare bees. Colonies of the Shrill carder bee (*Bombus sylvarum*) with its famed high-pitched buzz, and the Red-shanked carder bee (*Bombus rudararius*) make the Burren by far the most important location for them in Ireland or Britain.

The Burren is an internationally important example of a glaciokarst terrain attracting geologists and wannabe-geologists. The Karst Working Group, made up of representatives of the Geological Survey of Ireland, the Geotechnical Survey of Ireland, the International Association of Hydrogeologists, and the Irish Association for Economic Geology, has produced an illuminating booklet, *The Karst of Ireland*, focusing largely on the Burren. Groups such as the Revue de Geographie de Lyon have explored and investigated the distinctive features of the limestone for their report: *Un région Karstique d'Irlande: Le Burren.*

In wetsuits, wellingtons and waterproofs, experts in vegetation, eminent scientists, and distinguished archaeologists come in thirst of knowledge. Experiments have been carried out to try to work out why there is such a unique mixture of plants. A professor from University College Dublin, Dr Bruce Osborne, has carried out work showing that plants have unusual reactions to water. His three-year study (2002–05) looked at the role of water availability and its effect on the plant community in the Burren. The study was funded to the tune of €220,000 by Enterprise Ireland along with money from the Environmental Protection Agency. The main species under consideration was wood sage, a sour herb that thrives where drought conditions are worst. At this stage photosynthesis is reduced and pores in the leaves, known as stomata, begin to close. The stomata are regarded as being crucial for plant survival because they open to allow in carbon dioxide for photosynthesis and they regulate water.

The ecological diversity of the place is astonishing. Scientists have frequently debated topics for weekends and weeks on end, teasing out the issues of the day. Groups of leading bryologists, whose interests cover mosses and liverworts, have met several times here for a knees-down. In July 1994, during a week of climbing the bluffs of the hills, searching little-visited limestone valleys, and exploring hazel scrub and rock crevices, the British Bryological Society recorded a staggering 195 mosses and 77 liverworts. The days of these obsessives are happily spent bryologising areas rich in epiphytes, finding *Neckera crispa* in abundance and discovering hepatics – notably in the Glen of Clab near Poulavallan, and south of Mullaghmore at Watts' Lough (named in honour of Professor W. A. Watts of Trinity College Dublin, who carried out palynological research in the area).

Plant ecologists have had many happy hunting days in the Burren. They come to probe the pattern of grassland and heath communities carrying out reviews of the distribution of the suites of rare plant species. In the words of the author David Jeffrey: 'A testable hypothesis is developed that explains the relationship between parent materials and vegetation distribution in terms of community dynamics'. Consultant ecologist Dr Grace O'Donovan first came to the Burren to carry out her doctorate at Mullaghmore on plant nutrient dynamics and has been visiting regularly ever since.

Environmental scientists have buried deep into the ground at Mullaghmore and Slieve Rua to investigate the legacy of the glacial soil. The appropriately named Professor Richard Moles has spent many years untangling a complex web of historic geological events. On Knockanes Hill, north of Mullaghmore, he found pieces of unweathered charcoal 2m below ground level dating from the mid-Bronze Age.

The Burren attracts people on highly focused quests. The celebrity chef Gordon Ramsay visited Ballyvaughan in 2008 to dive for edible sea urchins at a secret location in the bay. European arboreal experts (otherwise known as self-confessed tree nuts) and mycologists have come to study a rare fungus – the glue fungus (*Hymenochaete corrugata*) on hazel trees in Keelhilla wood in the Burren National Park. It is found in only a few locations elsewhere in Europe. Their fascination with it is because it glues dead hazel twigs to living branches in the canopy, thus preventing them from falling to the ground where they would be available to other fungi to decompose. In turn, hazel trees have themselves come under much scrutiny. Research fellows have studied land-use change looking at the effects of the cessation of grazing and the spread of hazel on biodiversity.

Archaeological digs at early medieval settlements and other locations throw up curious ancient treasures. The first decade of this century has produced more than its share of significant finds. Remains found in large quantities in scores of the Burren's caves have included those of a wild cat, which, until it was discovered, was not known to have existed in Europe. The Department of the Environment, Heritage and Local Government has funded excavation at Glencurran cave in the Burren National Park. The work, led by the Sligo Institute of Technology, took place during part of 2004–05 and 2008–09. The crouched trowellers uncovered almost 40,000 animal bones and bronze fragments, more than 500 artefacts and 100 human bones. In 2010 the archaeological team at Glencurran dug up a 1,500-year-old Viking necklace, the largest ever found in Ireland. The archaeologists believe it may have been traded between Vikings in Limerick and Gaelic chieftains in the Burren. It was described by the leader of the dig, Dr Marion Dowd, as 'stunning'.

During the summer of 2009 archaeologists were, in the words of Graham Hull who was quoted in the press, 'jumping up and down at the discovery of a stone arrowhead' at Caherconnell stone fort. It was believed to date to approximately 2500 BC and could be the Burren's oldest habitation site. At the same location in 2007 a ten-day excavation unearthed an Edward I silver halfpenny dating from 1300 AD to 1310 AD. During a dig at Kilcorney, near Kilfenora, in April 2003 the bones of a prehistoric woman and her baby were recovered. In 2000, the Irish Stone Axe Project (ISAP) uncovered near Doolin a pale green stone axe which suggested a link between Neolithic people in Ireland and Britain. Petrological analysis showed that it was of a type of stone known as 'tuff' which is typical of tools produced in Cumbria.

~~~

As a mere scribbler I do not pretend to understand much of the impenetrable scientific terminology written by experts in their field. The tone of some of it is stiff in manner, the language cold, and it has a narrow focus specialising in hard facts. It can be difficult navigating the labyrinth of the complex and stodgy prose. Reading some of the archaeological reports makes me aware of a timescale that strains the imagination. This is not in any way to belittle the formidable battery of scientific knowledge and academic exactness, as well as the usefulness of the work in illuminating the subject for future scholars.

The purpose of the foregoing pages is to show a flavour of the remarkable breadth of research – largely unknown to any but the most dedicated groups. It represents only a small amount of the type of work being carried out and does not even begin to scratch the surface. But it is a reflection of the infinitely fascinating surroundings and of how the Burren can profoundly affect and entrap those on specific missions. I never lose my sense of wonder at their enthusiasm, their undisguised pleasure in their subject, their passion, bordering on fanaticism, and their dogged ability to produce new material and conjure up new facts at which, like watching the journey of a beetle across a rock, all we ordinary mortals can do is marvel at the extraordinariness of it.

When I discovered the long, unforgettable Latin binomials (the two-part names that denote a species) for the wild flowers I was immediately captivated. Who could resist *Geranium sanguineum, Dryas octopetala, Gentiana verna, Orchis masula, Neotinea maculata, Dactylorhiza fuchsii, Minuartia verna, Armeria maritima, Lotus corniculatus, Rosa pimpinellifolia* and dozens of others? There is a seemingly endless variety of flowering species. Once you have mastered their names the next challenge is their pronunciation. As a long-time insomniac, instead of counting sheep, I have found it a relaxing exercise to run through an incantation of them under the duvet. I usually fall asleep before I have reached one of the longest of all, the 26-lettered *Tripleurospermum maritimum* or the 25-lettered rhyming *Chrysanthemum leucanthemum* with their evocative reduplicated endings.

There is colour in the flowers, but also a magical colour in these botanical names. I have often wondered about their provenance. How did they come about and who were the taxonomists who dreamt them up? The famous biologist Carl Linnaeus started the ball rolling when he published the definitive edition of his

Systema Naturae in 1737. To this day biologists rely on his rules to identify the living things around them. Taxonomists are the experts who have named and described nearly one and half million of the planet's living and extinct creatures and plants. The names at first seem a confusing jumble, more reminiscent of the look and the length of places in Gwynedd in Wales. Part of the fun of each visit is remembering them and relating these to the more well-known English versions. Little wonder an elderly man that I once met walking along the Flaggy Shore told me that the flowers 'all have outrageous names'.

Tourists on shoreline at Black Head © Marty Johnston

3

The Pool of Sorrows

The bones of this land are not speechless.
So first he should learn their language,
He whose soul, in its time-narrowed passage,
Must mirror this place.

Frances Bellerby, 'Artist in Cornwall'

New York has its Statue of Liberty, Moscow its Kremlin, Pisa its Leaning Tower, London its Big Ben, and China its Great Wall, but the image that represents the Burren is a megalithic monument tucked away inland. Baffling yet strangely familiar, the Poulnabrone portal dolmen is a lodestone that has spawned a million photographs. From the black and white days of the heavy whole-plate camera and box brownie, through the Vest Pocket Kodak (VPK) years of the 1940s and 1950s, to the digital colour exponents of the twenty-first century, scores of trigger-happy Nikon visitors have felt the call to capture this arrestingly visual image and click their photographic stuff.

They are now photoshopped and equipped with tripods, ultra wide-angle long lenses, metres, filters, lights, image-stabilisers, reflectors, diffusers, polarisers and fast exposures, taking pictures at a resolution of about seven million pixels and agonising over shutter speeds. The dolmen has been photographed from every possible angle in every possible light, in every possible season with every possible camera, at all hours and in all colours: radiant and burning, frozen, grey, lunar, red, white, yellow. Looming up dramatically with its enormous roof slab, or capstone, it is a conspicuous structure that possesses a characteristic brilliance, startling casual passing motorists. Driving past, even for those with only the slightest smidgeon of curiosity, is not an option. Marooned on an acre or more of flat and open pavement, the setting of Carboniferous limestone gives it character and liveliness.

In the literature and cultural heritage of the Burren, it is a leitmotif. It corresponds to everyone's idea of the traditional dolmen – a stone table resting on pillars. Leafing through guidebooks and breathless tourist promotional fliers throws up many superlatives: dramatic, breathtaking, magnificent, spectacular, astonishing, mighty, majestic and awesome are just a few applied to it. Whichever single adjective is used, Poulnabrone has entered the collective imagination as a potent part of the fabric of the landscape and a globally recognised name. Its silhouetted outline is to be seen everywhere: on postcards (artistic, humorous and mythical) calendars and t-shirts, on magnets, menus, mugs and mouse mats, and on the walls of pubs, hotels, B&Bs and cafes. Everywhere, it cuts a recognisable and sometimes Celtic-twilight figure, often with swirling multi-coloured energy patterns above it. You will find its image exoticised as a logo all over Ireland: in tourist information offices, gift shops, pitch-black on glossy book covers (Irish, spiritual, and touristic, often with dramatic clouds moving across the sky), framed pictures, holiday brochures, walking guides, soft-focus on CD and DVD covers, and gracing countless Irish travel articles as well as advertising features in newspapers and magazines. The 'Kodachrome dolmen' has unknowingly won more prizes and ribbons in camera club competitions than any other outdoor feature of the Irish landscape.

As an emblematic flag, it has featured in poetry and music, as well as on an Irish postal service stamp and once made an appearance on the Irish Oatmeal biscuits box. The craft workers at Mullingar Pewter have cast a fine grade replica of it (€350 for a large and chunky version, €69.95 for the smaller one). In autumn 2010 as part of a public art initiative, an American artist, Jim Ricks, created an inflatable version called the 'Poulnabrone bouncy dolmen', twice the size of the original. He wanted to produce a soft playful symbol of post-Celtic tiger Ireland and for him bouncy castles represented an icon of contemporary society as much as Poulnabrone was an icon of ancient Ireland. Using a high-powered fan, the dolmen inflates in minutes and is designed for all age groups. The purpose of it is to engage creatively with communities in the Slieve Aughty Mountains, an area east of the Burren, and a place bereft of dolmens.

Despite the inflated hyperbole and the fact that it is the most photographed, sketched, painted, talked and sung about megalithic tomb in Ireland, it still manages to possess a magical quality at whatever time of day and whatever time of year. Even on the coldest winter's day a few cars are generally parked beside it while the occupants meditate on this megastar amongst dolmens. It is a short walk to reach it across the pavement and visitors gravitate towards it by a magnetic pull. For many it is simply a tourist curio that they have read about and feel they must see, paying homage with a cursory ten-minute wonder and wander amidst its archaeological past and a thirty-second camera pan.

Others arrive with a thirst that needs quenching. To them it is a source of mystery and reverence. They frown and poke their way around it with a look of bemusement or bafflement as they try to fathom what it is and tease out some of its meaning. Promises and engagements have been made at this place of assignation – a mystical spot to seal a future life together. But mostly it is a staging post for tourists on an Irish whistle stop (frequently more whistle than stop as a tour leader once told me) must-see heritage hit list that includes the nearby Cliffs of Moher, the Blarney Stone, Yeats' grave, Newgrange megalith tomb, and the Giant's Causeway. In 2009 Failte Ireland used its image for the cover of 'The Seven Wonders of Ireland', a brochure selling it as one of the most spectacular places to visit with free admission. A tourism visitor survey showed that during the summer, 2,000 people a day visit the site; the average length of time spent there is ten minutes. Tourist board estimates put the number of people viewing it each year at more than 100,000. This means that in the past twenty years, potentially, 2 million people have stopped at the site.

I have watched visitors arrive with cameras slung around them, bouncing on their oversized bellies, hell-bent on sightseeing. They fiddle with lenses and focusing, posing, loitering for a few minutes, waiting for a shift in the light, checking their filters, worrying about focal length measurements, surveying the hugeness of the sky, hoping for the rain to stop, the sun to reappear, or for a crescent moon, or pacing around to secure the sunset's image sharpness for the 'decisive moment'. A quote from the seventeenth-century Cardinal de Retz: *Il n'y a rien dans ce monde qui n'ait un moment decisif*, 'There is nothing in this world that does not have a decisive moment', and a concept associated with Henri Cartier-Bresson.

Solitary botanists wander around it in a private communion with some rare arctic or alpine species. On numerous visits I have noted burnet rose, vetch, twayblade, wild thyme, lady's mantle, tormentil, milkwort, daises and primroses. Other visitors circumnavigate it, shivering in their fleeces, staring underneath as their eyes travel up and down, listening attentively to their guides, then asking: What is it about?

So what is it they have come to see? What is the appeal of this neatly arranged tableau of stones? The name Poulnabrone, *poll na mbron*, which is sometimes spelt Poolnabrone, is said to mean 'the pool, or pit, of sorrows'. But in *Burren Journey* George Cunningham suggests it means 'the hole of the querns' since 'brone' comes from the Irish word 'bro' meaning quern. Other interpretations say it means 'The Hollow of the Millstone'. The dolmen itself is a simple form of chambered tomb made up of slender stones supporting the elongated, steeply-tilted roofed capstone measuring 3m by 2m. It was built 5,800 years ago. The term portal dolmen is believed to be a derivative of court tombs. Most contain only a single chamber while others have two. The grave goods associated with them are similar to those linked with court tombs. Down the years it has suffered weathering wear and tear and at the hands of graffiti artists.

In 1985 a visitor spotted a spiral crack in the eastern portal stone which worsened through time and meant that urgent conservation work had to be carried out. During 1986 and in 1988 archaeologists excavated the chamber. Professor Ann Lynch, who carried out the work, noted that the excavation of the chamber showed much about the form and structure of the tomb. The sill-stone at the entrance was sitting in an east–west gryke, forming a natural socket. She found that some soil was incorporated in the cairn matrix and several large stones had been placed on edge in grykes to help stabilise the structure.

During the excavation, fragments of human bone were recovered from throughout the chamber deposit. Thirty-three bodies – seventeen adults and sixteen children, male and female – were found along with their grave goods which included ornamental beads, two quartz crystals, a miniature polished stone axe, pottery and a triangular piece of bone perforated by eleven circular holes. The artefacts recovered also included the tip of a flint or chert arrowhead found embedded in the hip bone of what was thought to be a man. It is believed they were buried at the site between 3800 BC and 3200 BC. Professor Lynch concluded that the majority of the adults died before reaching thirty while only one lived past forty. It was found that the eastern portal stone was cracked beyond repair and was replaced with a stone cut from the pavement. The experts also decided that since the weight of the capstone was being supported by just three stones, an extra support was necessary on the western side of the chamber to spread the load more evenly. A new modern replacement stone was inserted in the gap between the two eastern chamber stones.

Many illustrious antiquarians and writers have visited the site. Thomas Westropp, an engineer and gentleman antiquarian, was a regular visitor to the Burren at the end of the nineteenth century and in the early part of the twentieth. In 1899 he took what is believed to be the first published photograph of what he called 'Poulnabrone Cromlech'. Given its age, it is remarkably clear, showing a tall man in hat and greatcoat complete with pipe standing erect beside the dolmen with a canny, curious glint as befits a Victorian scholar. Westropp also sketched the dolmen and wrote about 'the airy poise of its great top slab, which, contrary to the usual practice, slopes towards the west'. A contemporary of his, George Victor Du Noyer, also sketched it, showing off its mound in fine detail.

Other writers have attempted to capture its spirit. In the 1960s, Richard Hayward called it 'a most impressive example of its class'. In an accompanying sketch in Hayward's *Munster and the City of Cork*, Raymond Piper's elegant drawing shows off the tilting capstone to great effect under a cloud-filled sky. Seán Jennett described the capstone as 'cockily asserting itself'; in his guide to the historic monuments of Ireland, the archaeologist Peter Harbison referred to its timeless simplicity 'rising like a bird about to take off'.

Besides its human history and animal analogies, rabbits have also penetrated into it. One afternoon I saw a hare standing guard over it, scampering around it several times before hastily taking its leave after sensing my presence. An enterprising farmer once attempted to charge people for access to this national monument but the pay-per-view system never took off and lasted only a number of weeks. In 2001 the State bought the site and 16 acres of land for €380,000 from a local farmer to help control access. It was the most expensive deal for land with exposed limestone pavement in the Burren. A newspaper report at the time quoted the landowner Tommy Byrnes of Newtown, Ballyvaughan, saying he was 'lonely parting with the dolmen, but happy now that the State will be able to give it adequate protection'.

As part of a €2.2 million European Union conservation programme over a five-year period from 2004 to 2009, eco-friendly cattle were moved on to the limestone to help control the spread of vegetation. The growth of scrub was seen as the dolmen's biggest environmental threat. The idea was that the cows would 'manicure' the land by controlling the scrub, which, in turn, would help increase the biodiversity and improve the quality of the nearby water. The cattle were brought in to graze the site several times a year and the scheme proved successful as well as giving tourists an unexpected photo-opportunity.

Around the same time, the marketing people were infiltrating the area to fill the vacuum of a lack of hard on-site knowledge with the erection of three lengthy, colourful information signboards – relatively tastefully done, as much as these can ever be tasteful. After all, the dolmen has stood uninterpreted for thousands of years until someone in an office suddenly decided what a good idea it would be to tell the public about its significance. In one swoop of a copywriter's pen a large element of the mystery and a little piece of the magic surrounding it is removed. No longer are visitors allowed simply to draw their own confusions. But they can still read it as they find it, tap into their ancestral yearning, and guess at its meaning. The dolmen creates imaginative possibilities; its distinctive shape has prompted many a simile and metaphor. It has fancifully been called a launching pad for a stone-age missile, likened to a primitive statue of an elephant, and the capstone compared to a giant's dining room table.

~~~

On a hot September day I chatted to some visitors from Chicago who had disgorged from their coach to survey the dolmen on what they excitedly called their 'power-sightseeing' tour of Ireland. Is this rock real? I heard one woman ask. One of the men, who introduced himself as Bert, referred to it as a 'Neolithic outhouse'. Gazing hard at me with a serious look, eyes squinting in the sun and just visible under a black baseball cap, he asked po-facedly: 'Did you know the guy who's buried here, friend?' He breaks into a wide smile and we get talking. Bert told me he was a retired engineer and draughtsman. The dolmen had, he said, 'knocked the socks off him'.

'It's kinda reassuring in a way, you understand what I'm saying, friend? We like old things and coming here to see your castles and dolmens have a great appeal for us.'

Jotting down figures in a notebook, he sets about a mathematical calculation working out its weight and sizing up its jagged geometry. 'Eight feet across by ten feet long and it's tapering . . . right? Say one foot thick – these are approximate . . . right?'

He puzzles, goes down on his hunkers to look underneath, and then stands on tiptoes scrutinising the capstone. 'I'd say there's eighty cubic feet in the roof and if we multiply that by the weight per foot, that works out roughly at one-hundred-and forty pounds plus by eighty equals eight thousand pounds, or four ton. That's an estimate but I can guaran-damn-tee you it's not too far out. You understand, friend? S'pity we couldn't speak to the people who built it.'

Before departing Bert produces his new slim trim Samsung camera and asks me to photograph him standing in front of the dolmen. 'It's got optical zoom and it's fitted with something called autoscene recognition which is just as well for me as I've trouble switching it on.'

Mellowed by time and weather, the site is now roped off to prevent tourists walking, crawling, patting, pawing, pinching, embracing, caressing and tape measuring the dolmen in a quest for its exact proportions. This has meant an end to the up close and personal, tactile 'stroke-me pleasure'. No longer can people stand on top of it or underneath it, pretending they are holding up the soaring roof stone by themselves. In 2009 the Office of Public Works appointed a full-time warden to keep an eye on the site. He told me that several teenagers once brought along golf clubs to tee-off while standing on top of the capstone. These antics led to it being roped off and mean that visitors miss out on the experience of the touchy-feely kamenitzas.

A small sign that has now been removed described it as a burial place of the 'special' dead. The meaning of special was not spelled out but archaeologists believe that because of the number of individuals interred here it can hardly represent a Neolithic community and must therefore be regarded as a special place. There is no human habitation but plenty of visitors. On an average summer's day you will hear a mix of transatlantic, European and Asian voices. Early one spring evening a young mid-west American woman was in thrall of the silence of the place. The only sound was the call of the cuckoo – described by Wordsworth as 'a wandering voice' – echoing across the limestone. I was struck by the sorrowful beauty in her face and watched as tears rolled from her eyes. I enquired as to what had caused her sad state. She had been travelling across Europe, she said, and was pining for home and her parents. The only cuckoo she had ever heard before was in the clock in her Minnesota home. For her, Poulnabrone was a true place of sorrows, a place of *lacrimae rerum*.

I too have lingered here, overdosing in the noiseless evening air as darkness descends and the cuckoo rinses the night air. The sun hangs tantalisingly behind the dolmen, then suddenly winks a farewell and the last of the light is snuffed out. In the rich afterglow of a moonlit night, there is a mystical feel. I reflect on the meaning and significance of this solemn and spectacular monument that has been a silent witness to many aspects of Irish history. I have often wondered how the builders managed to raise the mighty capstone into position, what inspired them and who they were. Whichever method they used must have been a considerable feat, manoeuvring and levering it on to the upright stones. The limestone flags supplied the builders with their raw materials so they did not have to carry it a long distance before erection.

But they still must have had to sweat. The ghosts of the builders are silent and although time has yielded a greater understanding there are still unanswered questions. The individuals who built it had their own reasons: was it chieftain, queen or priestess, and why did they choose this specific location? Did they regard it then as a sacred landscape? Was it a place with magical powers? No written records exist from the time, so speculation surrounds the answers to these and many other riddles. The attraction of the place is the mystery and guesswork, and the fact that no one knows the dolmen's exact tonnage, its spiritual or social significance or the reasons for the numerous artefacts that were uncovered in the 1980s.

In an essay 'Stones in Seventeen Frames' about the *Maen Ceti* burial chamber in the Gower peninsula, Wales, Menna Elfyn discusses how these ancient builders worked:

> *Conspirato* is what was needed to raise that twenty-five-ton enigma of a capstone. The company of others to breathe together, to conspire. A tug of stones. That lift of common imagination.

Under a sickle moon, there is an inscrutable whiff of secrecy and eeriness about being abroad and alone at night. Occasionally a car passes, its lights throwing up a gleam on the roadside momentarily breaking the darkness. Aside from this there is no noise. It is a place of cathedral-like silences and sorrows. Rooted to its grandiose solitary spot, it stands as an exquisite sculptural set piece with a sense of timelessness. There are times I feel sorry for it, yet its ego seems to carry it and the reputation of its image precedes it. It speaks across the centuries and has stood through thousands of winters with generations of legends and mythology wrapped around it. On numerous visits I have never felt lonely here, perhaps only ever experiencing an occasional charge of the melancholy that is inherent in the air.

Over the years dozens of knee-high doorway-shaped mini Poulnabrones have been erected all around by visiting twenty-first century freelance megalithomaniacs to emulate the mother of all dolmens and keep it company in the long dark nights. Some of the small dolmens built here have been arranged with care. They resemble the style and embody the spirit of the mysterious stone figures known as inuksuit found throughout the Arctic. For the Inuit, theirs are objects of veneration defining the geography of the spiritual landscape. The Inuit look through these rectangular-shaped windows to see if there is a sightline which may have been intended by the builders.

No one can say with certainty the intention of the Poulnabrone builders. But there it stands, self-confidently embedded on a grassy mound, a primordial prima donna among dolmens, an exuberant head-turning show-stealer, a cynosure casting its spell and attracting its own band of paparazzi resembling at times a gallery jostling at a film premiere. Sanctified by several hundred years of sightseeing and wave after wave of humans, it has achieved celebrity status and a pulling-power all its own.

As a posse of German visitors prepares to leave, they steal one last glance on their way back to their minibus. Before departing from the drystone wall at the roadside, they align the Big One in their camera lens. Time for one last photo-opportunity of an enduring totem, one final mass salvo of clicks, a mini orchestra of digital technology filling memory cards, accompanied as dusk descends by theatrical flashes of light. One man wearing a white jersey with 'Deutschland' in black lettering on the back performs a 360-degree pirouette, twirling slowly on one foot with all the precision of Rudolf Nureyev, capturing the dolmen in its surrounding wider limestone home. He proudly produces his Coolpix Nikon camera pointing out its intelligent sweep panorama button and triumphantly showing me his image.

The best times to shoot the dolmen are at dusk and dawn, during what photographers call the 'magic hours'. Before boarding their bus, the Germans review their images on the LCD screen, talking of the publishing possibilities it offers. If the photographs that have been taken here over the years were laid out, they would cover millions of square metres. In an area with scores of wedge tombs, ring forts, and cashels to choose from, Poulnabrone is incontrovertibly unassailable. In any dolmen hall of fame, its unique overwhelming presence distinguishes it from the mass of others. There is no contest. Its attachment to the Burren is age-old, permanent and inseparable.

It is a place, not only of unceasing wonderment, but also of romance, mystery and flash photography. On each visit it is good to have been here, to have been spiritually uplifted and have spent time loitering in this pool of 'photogenic' sorrowness. There are few better places to watch the evening light congeal in a site for the special dead, blessed with a special virtue, in the bosom of the Burren and in a place some call the soul of Ireland.

Facing page: Poulnabrone dolmen stone in evening light © Marty Johnston

4

A Tour through the Paint Box

To know a physical place you must become intimate with it.
You must open yourself to its textures, its colours in varying
day and night lights, its sonic dimensions. You must in some
way become vulnerable to it. In the end, there's little difference
between growing into the love of a place and growing into the
love of a person.

Barry Lopez, *Extreme Landscape*

The colours, smells, sights and sounds work subtly on the
imagination. Sometimes they are striking or symbolic.
Our journey starts with the visual treats found on a colour-
questing tour in some unlikely places. The spectrum of colours
interlocks in a collage of greys, blues and greens, which are the
three that remain constant. You will find prismatic flowers,
sometimes offering striking contrasts in tone and an intriguing
juxtaposition. A walk through the paint box is a lesson in colour
geometry but some days it can seem as if there is no living colour.

In the Burren's hierarchical colour supremacy, grey
dominates. From a distance, there is a solemn monochromatic

mutedness to the limestone. The grey outdoor architecture can be either boring or fascinating, depending on your point of view. It can be difficult to come up with the precise colour description but in some lights it looks bleached-out, a landscape divested of technicolor. At first sight it is overwhelming in its teeming uniform greyness: pale grey, or ash grey as opposed to the darker grey of charcoal featured in clouds. Sometimes, as the light works its special effect, it becomes a greyish white or even greyish blue. There are myriad greys. On different visits, in different seasons, my notebooks contain descriptions of the analogous greys, a symphony in shades offering a galaxy of greys that would enhance the tint range in any paint company's chart: battleship or dreadnought, gunmetal, dove, smoke, a dull pewterish, platinum, the shade of elephant skin, the hue of a pigeon's breast, or the plumage of a heron or curlew. The depthless grey of a sombre sky accompanied by a murky cloak of mizzle adds another dynamic. On sunless days, with a lack of cheer, you want to shake a view out of the impenetrable greyness but the stubborn mist will not allow you. The hills remain undercover, the walls motionless.

There are times when the top layers of hillside terracing have a rutilant or purple glare and the visitor looking at it for the first time mistakes it for swathes of bell heather. At other times it is an incandescent, glowing light. Long after each visit it is grey – a calm, often cool or neutral grey – that overpowers as a colour imprinted in the mind. In terms of the equipoise of land, sea and sky, the palette consists of only three colours: grey, grey and grey. Only when it is contemplated in its assorted moods does the visitor discover that far from being monochromatic, the landscape is polychromatic.

Mother Nature has been generous with the Burren greenery and impressive eruptions of green corridors form everywhere. This pigment even has its own name. Spend long enough walking in the dark evenings across the fields around Ballyvaughan and you will eventually stumble across a spectacular moth first caught in 1949. The Burren green (*Calamia tridens*, subspecies *Occidentalis*) is a lime-green, inch-long species that delights photographers and naturalists alike. It is an apt – if slightly parochial – name for a striking insect. It was discovered near Gort by Eric Classey from London who organised the first entomological expedition to the Burren. He died in 2008 and, because of his Burren find, merited a generous obituary in the London *Independent*.

Verdure transforms the land freshened by rain but in all its multifarious shades, green plays second fiddle as the colour that overpowers after your eyes have switched from grey. Viridescence is round every corner and to the fore on the drove or green roads. It takes over from the minutiae of the wild flowers. Ferns, mosses, holly, grasses, hedges, bracken and the verdant drapery of trees produce a gallery of green: every shade to please chlorophilia addicts from bottle to pea, and from the bright and glittering dark green tumbling cascades of ivy to the exuberant green leaves breaking out on the twigs of beech trees and the pastel green of the young hart's-tongue fern. The woods throw up sticky-looking green spindle, an olive-green on the oak leaves, the darker green of juniper bent in the winds, the bristly green leaves of wild madder with straggling stems, the glossy green and treacly-thick deep green of the vegetation, or the stunning bright green of a field that stands out at Muckinish. On a clear summer's day of strong sunshine the gentle, dappled rays filter through the hazel trees on the lower slopes of Eagle's Rock at Keelhilla lighting up harebell with greenery ranging from the shade of the insides of cucumber to lovat.

The alchemy of new life in the spring recapitulation brings with it a mix of floral associations speckling the ground with a kaleidoscope of cheerful-looking colours straight from a

Summer sunset over Galway Bay © Marty Johnston

Top: The spring gentian, the emblem of the Burren © Marty Johnston

Bottom: Early Christian churches of Oughtmama © Trevor Ferris

Early-purple orchid – a Burren spectacular © Marty Johnston

The Flaggy Shore © Trevor Ferris

pointillist's palette. When you examine the detail of nature's infinite subtleties of shade and small rock flowers, and only when you get down on your knees, do you truly begin to appreciate the range, combination and collisions of resplendent colours clinging stubbornly to the limestone. Some are grouped tightly together in clusters of ten or twenty. Like sun-kissed, freckled, happy children, they thrive with an appearance of healthiness and luxuriance. They are delicate and extremely rare flowers, yet there are thousands, mass-produced it almost seems, for the tourist market. Sometimes towards the tail-end of spring and before the proper onset of summer, a few last lingering ones look weather-worn but pick the right moment and, like Tiffany's jewellery with the dissonances of daring colour combinations, the majority will bedazzle you.

Without warning, the vibrant blue of a spring gentian will stop you in your tracks. It is the Burren glitterati, a diminutive but spectacular blue that patterns the grass or limestone. It comes piercingly, like a bolt out of the blue, its five petals arranged around the mouth of a short trumpet. Blue, it is often said, is the rarest colour in nature. I have a passion for blue flowers. The tiny, pale blue common milkwort is found all over the Burren. Germander speedwell has bright blue flowers while the sky-blue harebell grows on road verges, limestone and in glades such as on the slopes of Eagle's Rock. Blue tick-lists include irises, asters and the Himalayan blue poppy, but none to rival the gentian – the blue petals of happiness. One of the Burren's most eloquent troubadours, the botanist Dr Charles Nelson, classifies gentian blue as the blue of the darker part of a clear summer sky at sunset – the colour that the Greeks gave to the eyes of Athena. He notes that not all spring gentians are like Athena's eyes – there are hues and variations of the colour; some are Cambridge blue veering towards turquoise or ice-blue and a few even paler. Whatever assortments of colour, they assert themselves with eye-catching vigour – an extraordinary blue. Gentians have a short life. One year, on 23 May (often said by botanists to be the key date to be in the Burren for the best spread of wildflowers) I saw more than a hundred in full flower over the roadside stone wall at Murroughtoohy North at Black Head; two weeks later returning to the same location, I discovered they had all folded.

There are smaller blues as well: bugle and the misty blue bordering on ultramarine of the sweeping carpets of bluebells in the woods as well as the powder blue of the Common Blue butterfly. The natural history writer Paul Evans says the colour blue always surprises. 'It knocks against the authority of white, pink and yellow and makes you look at the tiny details of the world with a fresh eye – it draws you in.'

Blue has a habit of overlapping with turquoise. Periwinkles found at Fanore have a blue tinge. The electric blue of damselflies jumps out at you when you are least expecting it. So too will the neon blue of a kingfisher, scarce here, but from the window of a B&B I glimpsed one on the River Fergus on the southern periphery of the Burren, darting past at high-speed in a straight line, flying low across the water.

Black Head and the sea surrounding it benefits from the benevolent light of the wide sky and sea. Stand here on a bright July day and, beyond the immediate stretch of pavement and rocks in front of you, the world is reduced to a blue horizon. There is a surfeit of sky. On cloudless days it is difficult to work out where the sea ends and the sky begins. But just as there are numerous shades of grey, so too there is a multiplicity of colours of the sea and its daily theatricality is restless and unpredictable. The processions of waves washing ashore have their own combination of moods. A typical Burren day ranges from calm, a quiet muttering, to flicks of waves, right up to a seething, roaring sea. The luminous colours are determined by the magnificent sky – the sky of all skies. Every minute, every hour, every day, each week, and in different seasons, the colours are changing. The coastal shallows, within a stone's throw of the rocky coast, are a different colour to the mid-ocean waters. The whole scene looks different from certain angles, from the sea, or from the sky. Scientists say that water absorbs any light that passes through it and sea-water absorbs the longer wavelengths of red and orange light more effectively than it absorbs the short, blue wavelengths.

Pale aquamarine morphs at certain times of the day into psychedelic shades of turquoise and a strong cobalt blue. Seen through the rain-saturated mist, the sea can look grey. At other times the waters give off a pale opal or a metallic appearance. Sea blues cover the blue paint box from the light hues of porcelain and powder blue to the Grecian blue of a fine summer's day. When it is on form, it can look blinding, like a glossy holiday magazine advertisement extoling the virtues of the waters around Santorini. On calm days it can seem to spread to infinity, a vast piece of still, blue-green silk with only an occasional gentle ripple, while other days it is an undulating silver with an aluminium-foil-covered look about it.

As you clomp across the limestone you will note flashes and tints of a ubiquitous burning golden yellow. After the dull winter months, many colour comparisons with the variety of shades of yellow are on show in the spring reawakening, harbingers of the coming summer: bananas, earth-moving equipment, a caged canary, a camembert sun followed by a big yellow moon and at other times a syrupy gold sun. Look closely and you will see evidence of the sheer intensity that Vincent van Gogh had in his paintings or on his wonky chair in Arles. There is the gorse almost turning to amber, and the fluorescent vividness of bird's-foot trefoil conjuring up in our minds a plateful of wholesome scrambled eggs. Elsewhere, expanses of kidney vetch, marsh marigold and yellow rattle vie for domination.

The hoary rockrose is as surprisingly bright as Ireland's *Golden Pages* telephone book. In places it competes in the annual yellow battle of the Burren flowers with the richly coloured wild iris in marshy fields and around the margins of lakes. Keep your eyes peeled and you will find ragwort growing abundantly on the limestone, and later in the summer a similar-looking plant called goldenrod with its flowers clustered in compact heads. Round every corner, bunches of the pastel yellow of evening primrose and buttercups flourish, reminding me of a riverside nature study walk at primary school.

The warmth of yellow, exemplified at its best in the summer morning sun, is cheery and in some cases surprising. It excites and creates an agreeable impression. Yellow and grey on the limestone sparkle in contrast. Visitors are often entranced by the brilliant yellow with a dash of orange-yellow of the Tortoiseshell, Brimstone, or Orange-Tip butterflies. Perhaps the warmth is found in a patch of jazzy dandelions in which honeybees plunge their heads deep between the florets in search of nectar or in a field-full of cowslips, celandines and primroses.

Through binoculars you may capture in sharp focus the hooked, yellowish beak of a cormorant rock-posing along the shoreline. You may also be lucky enough to catch sight of the pale lemon-yellow underside of the nimble grey wagtail on the roof of a house as it makes a balletic leap through the air, then twisting and flying in long bounds. Or you may exchange glances with a male blackbird looking up from its foraging, its yellow bill and eye-ring a similar colour to the gorse.

In some instances yellow can appear mellow when a flaxen, pallid light spills across a valley. On these days the tawny gold patina of hay bales and July grasses seen in the fields around Ballyvaughan appears to have a kinship to yellow. And what of the association with yellow in the Burren names? Aillwee means 'yellow hillside', and Aillwee Mountain has its own yellow to live up to its etymology. The walking man directing you along the green roads is painted a welcoming yellow; in winter some leaves on trees give off a radiant yellow. As they go about their winter work with only a few hours of daylight, the road sweepers bring their own dayglo variation to boreens and byways. And in the village, the Rent-an-Irish cottages show off an appealing yellow trim to their windows and doors.

A farrago of reds ranging from the overlap of strong pink seen in roses through the amber glow at twilight to deep burgundy verging on purple, bursts out in odd places. Like scarlet lakes, the ravishing red of the tall poppy lines roadsides. The plum red of fuchsia (that becomes a ruby red later in the year) and the orange-red of montbretia seen in ditches compete with each other for red devil supremacy. The scarlet of valerian, common all around the Irish coastline, is found in the northern Burren along roadsides and on walls. On an afternoon bike ride I once stumbled across a pulsating, solid mass of vivacious, beetroot-red flowers near Bell Harbour. The whole field was animated. I could not put a name on them but there were thousands by the roadside stretching across the pavement, revelling in the bright sunshine, in wondrous harmony with the limestone.

A fiery ocean sunset, complemented with clouds of deep crimson, is one of the evening delights. The dissolving sunset takes you through variations in the scale of reds: angry red rays indicating too much water vapour in the air through vermilion and deep salmon and plum dipping into amethyst. Late one summer evening outside Linnane's bar on the Flaggy Shore as I cradle a raspberry-jam-red glass of assertive New Zealand Oyster Bay Merlot, the western sky appears on fire. For more than thirty minutes I watch the dying of the fierce light. A ball of sun is sinking below the medium high clouds that are shaped like a gigantic mushroom with a bright red ring around them. Slowly, the sun sinks into the sea, the flaming red of Marie

Rua's hair. The clouds look like a smoking volcano erupting. Gradually as the temperatures drop and darkness sneaks across the hills there is a brief period of brightness in the reddening sky before it dissipates into black while Galway Bay melds into the first twinkling lights on the Connemara shore. More lights flicker into action; some a much brighter wattage than others: amber, orange, white form an elongated necklace from Galway city along the coast with occasional gaps between villages. Looking down on it all, a solitary, glowing star is accompanied by a bright, slender moon.

Other reds nibble-noted in my journal: seen close up, the blood-coloured wings of the red admiral is an electrifying red as it performs an aerial ballet; sometimes the sun is a dull, red bar down in the west; alizarin is the red colouring of madder, a herbaceous plant with yellow flowers. Best seen in grykes set against the limestone, the magenta of bloody cranesbill is one of the most striking and celebrated of all Burren flowers, and when the sun and the mood are right, it is a deep, rich claret; the bright red of wild strawberries growing at the deserted village of Creig; the red of the rusty-back fern; the blood red of the robin's breast; segueing into purple are the shiny autumn red fruits found on rowans, guelder rose, holly, spindle and blackthorn.

Purpling time in the summer catches the last of the pyramidal orchids and incorporates knapweed, thistles, buddleia and heather. The purple-pink wild marjoram with its bushy and erect leafy stems floods the roadside hedges around Rathborney in August. Sea pea along the shore near New Quay produces a stunning purple, while in the low December sun you can occasionally see a soft purple tint in trees that have shed their greenery.

Mid-May is a unique moment in the life of the Burren. On every track, and from every vista, hundreds of bright snowy-white flowers confetti the verges loading the spring hedges.

Road tunnels of high hawthorn trees flaunt a sparkling, frothing mass of floating castles of whiteness. The fragile white hawthorn set against a blue sky is a memorable moment.

White is the sum of all the colours in the spectrum. Butterflies that flit in and out of the hedges produce their own spectacular shade of white. Along the narrow road leading to the Martello Tower on the Flaggy Shore on a morning of glaring sunshine I followed the directionless flight of a Large White. Soon, more than twenty were flirting freshly, too busy to take time to settle on one flower. A mating pair whirled past locked together at the tail, white on white, exquisite Burren eye candy.

The creamy white flowerheads of mountain avens (*Dryas octopetala*) sparkle in the sunlight, sometimes looking more ivory-silk than cream. Thousands congregate in clumps along the roadside at Aghaglinny on the way to Black Head. In the townland of Gleninsheen vast swathes of dryas and trefoil cover a mixed area of grass and limestone across to Aillwee Mountain. Along the uncut verges of roads and lanes, in shady woods, grassy hillsides, rocky outcrops, and on the pavement you come across these flowers in abundance, while the white cumulus of cow parsley, growing extravagantly along hedges of the single-track road to Carron, contrasts with it. Colonising many areas of disturbed ground you will also find a spray of bright, white rays fringing the yellow eye of the tall ox-eye daisies.

On certain days the hills glisten with sparkling caster-sugar whiteness; at other times they have a chalk-white appearance. From a distance they give off a shimmering snow-radiance. The whiteness disappears on dank, lifeless, winter days, but on crisp and crunchy ones the hills look dusted with a frosty sheen resembling fondant icing. On sharp, icy cold days your breath appears white in the air.

The Burren's animals often speak of white. Our tour encompasses the washing-powder white of the feral goats roaming the hills, and the doves at the entrance to Aillwee cave which explode at times looking a white that is unnaturally sparkling. Whites are linked to the sea: the milky white flecks cresting the tops of the waves at Poll Salach, and the emulsion lily whiteness of the lighthouse at Black Head. Along the coast at Gleninagh, the hankies tied to branches of an ash tree have cauliflower whiteness. Turn over whelks on the beach and you will see a pearl-white interior; and each month, bearing down on it all, a full moon rises in radiated whiteness, bordering on the yellow of candlelight or buttermilk, as ascending plumes of white smoke rise from the cottages.

~~~

Catch a clear spring evening around half-past nine and you will be enchanted by one of the strangest of all effects that the Burren affords: a delicate, pale pink hue creeping imperceptibly across the rocks, rouging them with sunset. It is a lustrous salmon-tinted glow that settles for a few magical minutes as a long banner of pink on the higher terracing of the hills and sometimes on the limestone plateau. Visitors coming across this spectacle gasp in amazement, holding their breath in wonder. Some people call it 'purple-pink' and it even veers towards lavender. The atmosphere is diffusely illuminated as evening light and the pink coming off the clouds drenches the landscape. Such a wistful moment, although lasting briefly, holds mystery; it is logged in my cerebral files.

Search carefully and you will find infinite nuances of a rhapsody of pink. Sit outside Monk's bar with your newspaper and post-prandial, and as night elbows day out of the way, let the soft, vaporous light wash over you. Gradually, as you read and sip, you will notice a pink luminescence stealing across the bay and a low sky slipping quietly into Ballyvaughan harbour. The residual cloud burns away the day's embers and the sky turns a sensuous rosiness taking on a bubblegum pink as moonlight slowly mingles with it.

Pink flora highlights include clusters of sea thrift with its distinctive globes of flowers on tall stalks above cushions of green leaves. Its shading ranges from the watery pink of strawberry milkshake, through salmon, flesh-coloured to a touch of peach and, at its fading stage, a shell-like colour with the merest flush of pink. Occasionally it glows to a shocking pink clinging to the coastal verges and on the high grassy banks overlooking the sea around the lighthouse. Mountain everlasting produces tinges of pink on its silvery back although its leaves are white. In its summer best, billows of burnet rose have turned from white to a delicate pink. Sea shells cover the spectrum from mouse-pink to powder-pink and from cerise to carmine-pink. Traces of pink tinged with lavender, verging on white-pink are to be found on the upper hood-petal and the two laterally extending side-petals of the bee orchid.

Inspect the rocks and erratics through a magnifying lens, and you will notice they house fragile, conspicuous lichen communities representing fascinating microhabitats with a coloration all their own. Lichens are not plants but are made up of what scientists classify as a symbiotic partnership of a fungus with a colony of algae or cyanobacteria. They make their living from chemicals slowly dissolved from the rock as well as nutrients from the rain.

Lichenologists have identified no fewer than forty colours and there are hundreds of species of lichen. A close examination of these reveals a feast of vivid splashes of colour embroidered in unlikely places, embracing a variety of tints and overlapping tones: pale white, cappuccino cream, a brown-green suffusion, blue-grey, glossy black, olive-green, peppermint green, purple and pink. Yellow scales lichen is widespread and variations of this colour are to be found: yellow-pink/yellow-grey/yellow-green with a flushing of egg-yolk yellow rosettes, vermilion and deep yellow. On some, an abstract yellow, bordering on butterscotch, is apparent; it is similar to a toffee-yellow and in others a deeper orangey-yellow with a soupçon of tangerine or lemony streaks.

Out of the greys of the water, sky and limestone, colours jump at you incongruously. Take the case of Pond House at Finavarra which was part of the Skerrett estate. Built in the nineteenth century on its own private tidal lagoon, it stands on a sheltered foreshore headland near New Quay. An English artist, James Moores, painted the striped base of the house as an installation using a computerised reduction of J. M. W. Turner's painting of Norham Castle. Painted in ice-cream colours, it consists of a blur of twenty-four bands of colour similar to a bar code to which the paint was then matched. A 2-mm hairline gap between each colour imparts chromatic depth and the paint has remained unscathed by the sea.

Browns come in dark and matt coalescing into orange, orange-brown verging on tawny, blazing orange and bright to rust-red. A medley of shades, depending on maturity and age, comes with wan biscuity colours akin to rich tea and fruit shortcake, verging at the other extreme to monk-brown or the colour of the Bourbon sandwich biscuit with chocolate cream filling. Brown brings its own particular mood. Earthy browns are found in the pebbles and stones at the Rine but you will also see white, grey, silver, inky black and obsidian black, while the beaches at Fanore and Bishopsquarter take on the colour of fudge. As a connoisseur of chocolate, the colour of cowpats has intrigued me. They range from the darkest end of the Bournville selection, through Cadbury's Tiffin shades to the lighter smoothness of Lindt & Sprüngli double milk. Sea shells that I have picked up on my walks have incorporated taupe, aubergine and beige.

In the depths of mid-winter the hills shine black with a wet, tar-like appearance. Many birds are linked to black: the tails of the kittiwakes look as though they have been dipped in black ink; the jet-black of the male blackbird, the immaculate black of the jackdaw, and the shiny blue-black of the magpie all showcase assorted blacks. Black Head, although you will find black stones here and black guillemots, is not black at all. A walk along a quiet road in the coal-black darkness of a Burren night is something you will not forget; likewise, to experience the blackout at the Doolin cave and see the free-standing stalactite, branded by its owners as 'the palest gleam in the darkest deep', is not to be missed.

One bitterly cold Saturday in November on a wet walk near Lough Murri on the Flaggy Shore I was startled by a series of bugle-like calls accompanied by a mix of snorts and squeaks echoing around the lake's edge. Gliding from reed beds a flotilla of swans cruised smoothly at a steady pace. Part of a larger water bird gang of paddling ducks and gulls, they exuded an aura of gentleness. The assembly included mute swans and a pair of rare black swans, an unusual sight in the Burren. They circled playfully pulling on water plants and upending several times. Gracefully they emerged from the water, straightening elongated necks, intertwining and turning heads, and presenting a noble and sociable appearance.

But soon it became clear that all was not congenial in this choreography of nature and the swans were far from amicable soulmates. After much preening, scratching and displaying of their wide, white underwings, the black swans' bitchiness in defining their territory manifested itself with a clamorous ruffling of feathers and nasty snapping. They were keen to show who was boss of this stretch of water even though they were outnumbered 50–1 by *Cygnus olor*. After ten minutes the black swans poked vigorously with their dazzling red bills, nipping at the bottoms and long pointed tails of their white-plumaged cousins, seeing them angrily off.

They then decided to parade on the grassy bank taking the higher swan-upping ground a couple of metres from me where I noticed their slate-like feathers. The misnamed mute swans emitted a loud hiss and a series of falsetto grunts as they drifted off to the safety of their nest deep in the reeds. Through the sleety November rain, the black bullies tumbled back into the cold water, regaining their regal composure. My attention was distracted skyward by the dramatic entrance at high speed of a line of four whooper swans coming in to land in the centre of the lake. Like a well-drilled unit and with the skill of experienced airline pilots they touched down seamlessly on the water, adding an exotic flourish to the winter lamentation on the Flaggy Shore.

For twenty years I have colour-coded my visits on the Folding Landscapes map. Like a child having fun with a new wallet of felt-tip pens, on each visit I circle the places I have explored, each year discovering previously unknown riches. I can date my Burren visits and identify the years by the colour-key on the map. The area around Ballyvaughan is multi-coloured. Other heavily shaded areas include Mullaghmore, Poulnabrone, Carron, Black Head, Poll Salach, and the Flaggy Shore. Abbey Hill and Corcomroe clash with a variety of reds and blacks representing much-tramped areas of limestone. Lesser-known places are circled half-a-dozen times: Sheshymore, Poulaphuca, Leamaneh, Oughtmama and Kilfenora. A few others feature only one or two colours. The map is torn, stained and Sellotaped, but embodies memories of familiar locations and the thrill of new-found ones; I call it my Burren Rainbow Map – my map of many colours.

Facing page: The Flaggy Shore © Marty Johnston

5

An Aphrodisiac of the Senses

May the light that turns the limestone white
Remind us that our solitude is bright.

John O'Donohue, 'A Burren Prayer'

Taking an imagined step back in time, as I occasionally
like to do, I have often wondered about the sound of
the huge glacier coming slowly from Connemara 15,000
years ago dropping its rocks across this part of Clare. Digital
technology did not exist to record the acoustics for the archive
but I can imagine that the grinding, growling and groaning, the
squeaking of the ice incorporated with rock, the whole shebang,
was a powerful noise. It carried debris and soil, rock and other
detritus, dropping the boulders in all sorts of odd places. Often
when I think of glacial travel I am reminded of Coleridge's 'The
Rime of the Ancient Mariner':

The ice was here, the ice was there,
  The ice was all around:
It cracked and growled, and roared and howled,
  Like noises of a swound!

An Aphrodisiac of the Senses

I think of the natural noises that have existed here for years. It is a place of few rivers or waterfalls, but listen carefully and you can distinguish numerous different notes in the water: the repetitious surge and slurp of the waves at the seafront slapping against the rocks; the roar of the Caher River in full winter spate as it tumbles over stones; the trickling Rathborney stream; gentle lapping of water on the lakes; the torrential drumming of the rain and hailstones flying off the rocks. The 'plop' of a duck landing perfectly on water is always a happy sound. As they flap into land with their triangular feet poised, it is amusing to watch their speed-break wings in action avoiding a crash-landing.

The susurrus of Burren winds whistle through the walls and round the headlands. Sustained bursts of winter winds last up to thirty seconds. I once counted a continuous blast of forty-four seconds. The soft strata of sound, such as gentle hissing and sighing of the wind moving through the trees, provides a contrast. Some nights it is without sound. Hailstone showers erupt with automatic ferocity for a short, sharp period too. Life pauses for a few minutes. Cattle stop drinking and eating, goats are mesmerised, people stand in doorways, cars pull over as their fast-speed wipers are unable to cope with the force of it. Then life returns, tractors trundle along the roads and the place regains its cloak of serenity as the birds reappear.

Uninterrupted by traffic or people, early morning is a delectable time to savour the Burren songbirds. One spring Sunday in May, on a circular walk around the hidden waters of Lough Rask and with an enchanting mist rising slowly from the calm water like a geyser giving off steam, I listened carefully to a fusillade of birdsong. Concentrating on pitch, timbre and rhythm, I filled five pages of a notebook with squiggles, and recorded what the lyrical writer on nature and the typology of landscape Jim Perrin calls 'the immediacies of bliss'.

Through the dawn light I was chorused firstly by the wren

71

striking up a tune with its machine-gun salvo of loud trills and shrills. Soon the short but explosive warbling of the blackcap is followed by the sharp, repeated, metallic *tea-cher, tea-cher, tea-cher* of the great tit. A hoarse woodpigeon, with its muffled but rhythmic *coo-cooo-oo-ing* and emphasis on the second syllable, vies with the strident and liquid territorial song of the robin, a random mixture of *tsiip* and *tseee*, piercing the air, reverberating through the trees and around the lakeside.

Farther along, an unseen and barely audible goldcrest sounding like a wheelbarrow in need of oil emits its soft *ziida-ziida* tinkle lasting just a few seconds. I pause to study through binoculars a willow warbler delivering, from high in an ash tree, its soft *hoo-eet* which increases in volume before its sweet string of descending notes fades and it departs to another tree. Languid and unmistakable, the call of the cuckoo carries far over the flat ground from neighbouring fields. The water birds of Lough Rask are also full of early energy. The contented chuckle of a mallard on the lake and its accompanying gentle splash-splash is disturbed by the flight of a pair of herons circling high with their *krarnk* call.

On my walk along roads filled with hedgerows and scrub, moments of minor drama animate the sky as birds go about their business. An agile swallow, on a fly-past, smartly sees off a harassing sparrowhawk and then continues its glorious jumbled twittering. A redpoll, with its distinctive trilling, undulates swiftly in the distance. Back in the slowly awakening village, the three notes of the song thrush *get up, get up, get up . . . go-to-bed, go-to-bed, go-to-bed* stir and confuse sleepy Ballyvaughanites. Elsewhere the shriek of a magpie, the repeated *chirp chirp* wake-up call of two gregarious house sparrows, and the insistent *grukk-grukk* of a pother of ravens gatecrashes the Sunday morning silence.

Frequently I am surprised at the profusion and diversity of

birdlife that can be heard, if not seen, in one small area. A few hours spent alone in the Burren serenaded by up to twenty birds is a lesson in the art of tuning in to a whole world of acoustic animal language and of appreciating the extraordinary symphony of sounds that only early morning can bring. Every year, as more and more common birds join the list of endangered species, it is something to celebrate, pure and unadulterated.

Useful mnemonics have often helped me in the fraught business of understanding the calls, communications and love notes of birds – happy, plaintive, harsh or lilting. But always, in trying to separate the chiff from the chaff, I take away the simple if sometimes frustrating pleasure of listening to competing tuneful songsters while at the same time trying to catch a glimpse of Lough Rask's avian rascals at their rhapsodic peak.

If you wish to turn off the ornithological soundscape, silence is easy to find. Sounds are concentrated in this place steeped in tranquillity. Pockets of stillness are everywhere and you can soak up the silences in numerous character-filled settings. Some places that spring to mind offer reflective space, inner peace and quietude: the top of Mullaghmore Mountain, a shaded glade at out-of-the-way Keelhilla far from traffic, Sheshymore's hidden pavement where the air is abnormally silent, Berneens townland where there is no human contact, the cliffs at Carron where the silence is all but absolute, and the soul-stilling Corcomroe Abbey where the silence listens to the silence but where, if you listen carefully, you may hear the monks chanting their vespers. For many visitors 'The Abbey of Our Lady of the Fertile Rocks', where Yeats set his play *The Dreaming of the Bones*, is one of the most placid of all Burren places.

Walk southeast of the abbey for an hour and further peaceful, ecclesiastical exploration is to be found at the ruins of the three Early Christian churches of Oughtmama (*Ucht Máma* 'the breast of the mountain pass'). Hidden in a hollow surrounded by a wall with trees and vegetation all set in a wider valley of limestone hills, this ancient monastic site associated with St Colman is difficult to locate. One September morning I set out to find it, negotiating an obstacle course of stone walls, electrified fences, farm gates and cow pats. My route crosses square fields with sturdy cows, shoulder high nettles and thick clumps of thistles and dandelions. A red tractor with a link box stands in the centre of one field. In the corner of another, a steel container, its lid held in place by blue twine says: Cashel's Creep Feeder. On the ivy-covered wall of a neat whitewashed cottage sits a black metal US Mail Box.

I tightrope-walk across the narrow edge of a rectangular water trough bridging two fields for my first glimpse of the roofless buildings – an astonishing site in a remarkable state of preservation set against the backdrop of the terracing. My unexpected arrival startles a woodpigeon which clatters through foliage. The churches are arranged in an east–west layout and their thick walls, more than 6m high, are decorated with yellow and white lichen. Chunky cyclopean blocks, some up to 1m in length, have been used in the south wall of the western church. In the nave of the largest church I crunch across pebblestones through an elegant but simple arch. According to a Dúchas noticeboard (the only sign of outside worldly infiltration) little is known of the history of the churches but it is thought they may have become less important after Corcomroe was founded. No reason is given as to why they were built here. The two smaller churches – one about 37m to the northeast – may have been places for meditation or prayers. A large plan of how the area looked in the twelfth century when a community of monks was based here shows a medieval mill-race to the east with evidence of house sites. In a corner of the wall a small font intertwined with odd animals looking like lambs has been carved and a twenty-first century fern grows from it.

An Aphrodisiac of the Senses

In her gazetteer *Forgotten Stones* Averil Swinfen writes that the stony outlines of the churches blend into the surrounding countryside and 'look as though they have grown up from the landscape'. No signposts direct you to Oughtmama; there are no easy paths leading to it and it merits only a brief mention on most maps. It is seldom visited but the time spent reaching it and in admiring its pulchritude is a reward for those who make the effort to find this place where the quiet is turned on full blast. If the Abbey of Our Lady at Corcomroe is the mother of serenity, then Oughtmama, hard-to-find and impossible-to-forget, is mother queen of serene.

The whine of police sirens or ambulances is rarely heard in the Burren but occasionally the volume control knob is turned up. Noisy music-filled pubs, and car hill climbs are two examples, but those who want to enjoy these sounds are there through choice. Sound levels generally below 20 decibels are becoming a rarity. Absolute silence is unlikely anywhere but many parts of the 388 square kilometres that make up the Burren have low decibel levels and in its own way the power of silence acts as a stimulus.

Animal sounds frequently surprise me on my rambles, punctuating the still air. While walking one afternoon on the limestone at Murrough, the air resounded with the discordant foghorn-like braying of a donkey that seemed to be in trouble but may just have been looking for attention. From nearby fields cows responded with loud bellowing. The noisy competition lasted for a full five minutes.

Touch is the most intimate sense. Over the years I have noted the feel and consistency of many flowers. Touch sensations are difficult to describe but my jottings remind me of the textures I have come across: hairy and sticky leaves on plants and trees, some fleshy or resinous, prickly thistles, a rubbery, fuzzy or glabrous feel of certain flowers.

Nelipotting, or walking barefoot, is one of the supreme Burren pleasures, preferably on a sunny day soaking up the feel of the limestone, which retains its warmth like a convector heater. Find a long patch, cast off your shoes and socks, revel in its smoothness, move quietly over the grey clints and it will live long in your well of memory. And as you touch, feel, smell and taste your way around the lanes and over the pavement – shod or unshod – you slowly realise the Burren is a terrain of the mind and spirit, a provocative multi-sensory aphrodisiac.

~~~

Of all the senses, smell is the most primitive. Kipling once noted, 'Smells are surer than sights and sounds to make the heart strings crack'. The smells of the Burren are linked to memory and emotion, serving as moments of reminiscence bringing out the qualities of a particular place. A visit to Keelhilla triggers a potpourri of woody aromas. There is a fetid scent of damp leaves and on warmer days, as insects hover, a rich leafy smell permeates the air. The early purple orchid, according to botanical experts, smells of cat's urine. On the limestone you will come across wild garlic, coconut-scented gorse, the tang of the salty sea air and seaweed. In places the pungent three-cornered leek may assail your nostrils; a farmer once told me the milk from his cows that feasted on the leek was undrinkable.

Set in a calm and isolated valley surrounded by ruined churches, holy wells and ring forts, along a single-track road north of Carron, is one of the most congenially fragrant experiences. Cross the door into the Burren Perfumery and the air is suddenly weighted with new scents. On the shop counter you may be amused and confused to find a small cup of loose Suma coffee, an organic medium roast blend with a strong smell. This, the assistant says, clears the nose and neutralises the switch as you shuffle-sniff amongst the plant-based fragrances on sale. Educate your nose with lavender and jasmine, cedar and lemongrass or fennel and mint. Choose between a warm and sophisticated fragrance or opt for a light summery one, perhaps absorbing the fresh orange flower scent found in the neroli and orange body and hand cream, or the cocktail of the Monoi Tiare flower coupled with jasmine.

Perfume-sniffing, like the connoisseurs and their wine, is an experienced business and here they blend their scents to produce a harmonious combination that is both relaxing and energising. It is also one that suits different times and moods of the day. Even through their attractive green linen wrapping and gold thread, some sweet-smelling soaps will transport you to a field of new mown hay or perhaps induce in you a fresh, fruity and zingy suggestion of citrus. As you browse the shelves of soya candles, creams and floral waters, you may detect a whiff of vanilla. The exotic mix of delicate and heady aromas, coupled with the alchemy of the experience, lingers in the nostrils.

Once you have had your fix of the flower power of perfumed petals and of one of the Burren's most sensuous of all treats, a tour of the smells would be incomplete without sampling the essence of the national bouquet. One of the most unmistakable smells is found in the rare whiskies displayed on the shelves of Ó Loclainn's bar in Ballyvaughan.

The Burren Perfumery's formula includes an alcohol base mixed with distilled oils and water, but for a contrasting distilling experience from the floral one and a world away from lavender sacks, the scent sleuth should round off the day by sampling some of these blends. Premium Irish whiskies, with all their complex flavours and smells, are listed in the bar's sixteen-page leather-bound whiskey menu.

Ó Loclainn's is a whitewashed mid-nineteenth-century bar with wooden tables, photographs, curios, and a mahogany clock that does not tell the correct time – a trait of clocks in the Burren's watering holes. It opens only after 9.00 p.m. (and on Sundays after mass from 12.30 to 3.00 p.m.) because Peter, who owns the bar, farms during the day. The head honchess Margaret, who runs the pub with him, is a woman of immediate friendliness and has agreed to help me identify specific smell and taste sensations. Originally from near Fermoy in north Cork, she came to work in Gregan's Castle Hotel in 1990. Six years later she married Peter and became absorbed by the bar's history.

'It goes back to 1848 when it was originally a hotel and a stopping place for horse coaches,' she explains as her eyes search the shelves for the best-smelling whiskies. 'Very little has changed in one-hundred-and-sixty years apart from some modifications in 1997 when we added on bathrooms and extended a little. It had a dual function as it was a bar and shop, and the wooden drawers would have contained sugar, tea and spices. It's small and intimate and that's the beauty about the bar, you get to know all the customers.'

It is a bright and balmy early summer evening in August but little light seeps into the bar. The dark-panelled walls, glass cabinets and shelves tightly packed with hundreds of golden bottles create an ambience that attracts large numbers of visitors. Margaret is happy to let me smell and taste some whiskies but warns that she may have to attend to customers every so often since it is likely to be busy. On the wooden counter beside the old-fashioned cash register and box for the Missions in Africa she sets up eight of the best.

'This first is a twelve-year-old Jameson which has a combination of spice with mild woody undertones.' The bottle label declares: 'Sweetly mellowed by age'. She uncorks it and thrusts it under my nose saying it has matured in an oak cask. I detect a strong sherry aroma and cocoa taste.

'In later years it has been matured in a cask and you get the sherry smells coming through. It has a lovely long finish as well.'

An English couple is the first to arrive. They order a pint of beer and a glass of red wine, sitting silently at a table in the corner listening to my personalised tour.

'We'll move on to a slightly older Jameson – the eighteen-year-old Master Selection. The nose of this produces a spicier, almost toffee-fudge smell with a hint of nuttiness. The thing you find about the whiskies that are older than sixteen is that they become more toffee-like and concentrated by virtue of the fact that they are in the cask for that much longer. You get more of a nutty note coming through.'

Two bearded Dutchmen walk in and order Guinness. She darts round the counter to serve them and deal with a query: 'How do you get to Caves of Moher?'

Margaret teaches during the day, and multitasks seven nights a week as barmaid, whiskey adviser, and one-woman tourist information dispenser on the Shannon region's attractions. She deals with their question, tops up the creamy head of the stout and hands them their change.

'Now from Jameson we'll switch to Midleton Very Rare, a Cork whiskey launched in 1984 and one of Ireland's most exclusive. It has a spicy bouquet along with herbal touches. This is a very popular whiskey and at €14 a shot it is quite expensive, in fact it used to be our most expensive. But it's a vintage that has been aged to perfection and is the blend of many whiskies coming from a variety of casks.'

When I sip it I notice a spicy smell with flora touches and a hint of fruits and honey. The bar is beginning to fill. A man from the Czech Republic: 'I stay two nights in Low-goose . . . and tomorrow want to go to Doaling, do I go down the Screwer cork hill?'

Margaret's brow furrows . . . 'Low-goose?'

'It is B and B here.'

'Awh . . . Logue's B and B.'

From the far south of Ireland to the extreme north-east corner of north Antrim, we uncork a Black Bush from the Bushmills distillery. This is a drink, she says, with cult status – a mingling of fruity, malty and nutty sweet sherry. 'It's the most popular because it sells at a reasonable price and is affordable. It is a good all-year-round drink with a distinctive full-bodied aroma.'

There is no doubting the full-bodied side to it and by now my tastebuds are tingling. Margaret then produces a Bushmills sixteen-year-old which has what the experts call 'three wood' maturation and finishing. It has been matured in a combination of American Bourbon barrels and Spanish Oloroso sherry butts for at least sixteen years. 'We sell two single malts, a ten-year-old Bushmills which has overtones of vanilla and honey, and this sixteen-year-old. It has a ruby red colour as it has been in the cask much longer and the result is a fragrant and honeyed almond smell.'

A party of Germans bustles in and orders five half-pints of stout: 'Ve are coming from Düsseldorf unt spenting a veek in zis part of ze vest of Ireland unt tomorrow ve are wisiting some of ze churches ruins here unt ve wery much vish to see Clonamnoisey.'

While she is serving, I pour some water into my drink from a small Tullamore Dew jug and feel an oakiness and dry fruity brush on the back of my throat. I admire a mirror advertising H. S. Persse's Galway Whiskey, 1815, Nuns Island Distillery: As supplied to the House of Commons. The walls are decorated with framed black and white photographs of local characters and faded newspaper clippings. A small candle flickers in a glass vase on a shelf above an oil-fired stove. On the wall hangs a framed Admiralty Chart of Galway Bay produced by the Hydrographic Office in 1850. Beside it is a 1924 timetable for the Galway Bay Steamboat Co. Ltd giving the times of the Steamer Dun Aengus for services to Aran, Ballyvaughan and Kinvara.

Back at the counter it is time for Powers twelve-year-old Special Reserve with a hint of perfumed oils and a honeyed aroma. 'The standard Powers would be aged about eight years. This one is very fresh and the twelve years gives it that much more flavour with spice, honey and perfume. As a celebration or a one-off occasion, the connoisseur likes this version . . .'

A Thai visitor interrupts: 'Can you tell me how to go Lisdoonfarout?' Margaret produces a map. 'I like to go for the mating season there . . . when that is?'

Unflappably, she picks up the story '. . . there's one interesting thing about this bottle – Powers Gold Label – as it has three swallows on it. John Power used to say that it should be drunk in three swallows: one, two, three . . . down the hatch.'

Not wishing to be rude to John Power, I obey his instructions swallowing it in three quick gulps. 'Now you've often, I'm sure, seen the turf drying on the side of the narrow roads in Connemara, so we'll try the Connemara peated whiskey. It is the only peated one that we stock. It's selling well and is made by the Cooley distillery in Dundalk.'

She pours it into what she calls a special 'nose-in-the-glass' designed to contain the flavour and inscribed with calligraphy script saying Connemara peated single malt. 'When you're talking about peated whiskies you have to wonder how the peat flavours the whiskey and that happens very early in the whole distilling process. A lot of tourists like it because it evokes the sense of Irishness that we are trying to get across and it's a big hit with the Americans as it smells of the Ireland of their imagination.'

On cue, an American couple: 'Ma'am, we feel we deserve one of your finest whiskies 'coz we've had an awesomely long day starting out from our hotel in Eerie Square in Galway, then on to Doonaguaire Castle, Cork-ker-com-crow Abbey, then the big doll-man, and then we went to . . .'

In between pulling, pouring, serving, and listening politely to American tourists' monologues, Margaret deals with a host of queries before returning to sniffing. My marathon whiskey-drinking and -smelling session is slowing up. I find the Connemara peated has an initial fiery edge on my palate that soon settles down. Relentlessly she pushes on.

'Green Spot is our house whiskey and this one is around eight years of age. It is mellow and triple-distilled like all Irish whiskies. There is some sweetness on the finish and it has a lively clean nose. It has been quite difficult to get your hands on it as it comes directly from the suppliers in Dublin but it's very popular and we sell it by the bottle.'

My heart strings have cracked and I begin to feel a small bit groggy. Twenty Scottish peaty whiskies remain untested. Margaret surveys the shelves and laughs. 'We have 400 bottles of whiskey which include some repeats so it's a lot of dusting every day. The one we have most of is Midleton Very Rare, which is one of the oldest.'

A Chinese woman, with a torn green Michelin map of Ireland, orders a 'grass' of beer: 'I try to get to Rimrick tomorrow – you show me how?'

The bar is crowded and Margaret is busy treble-jobbing. She remains unflustered and wants me to smell some Scottish whiskies. I'm suffering a bout of MEGO: My Eyes Glaze Over. 'I've a couple left out here for you. Laphroaig from Islay is a single malt ten-years-old. It is a deep gold colour as you can see and is powerful on the nose.'

A long smell shows evidence of its smoky and tangy nature. 'It has seashore salt and earthy aromas. You'll notice it has a considerably different smell to the Irish whiskies with different scent because of the water that they use and the amount of peat.'

It is getting difficult to differentiate between the whiskies.

Coconut tastes blur with chocolate and caramel. 'The other one is Oban which has been matured for fourteen years. It's strong but not as overpowering and has a fresh, delicate hint of peat aroma with a long, smooth finish.'

At the end of our session Margaret talks about her own taste in whiskey. 'If I was out somewhere special I would take a Bushmills single cask which encouraged me to buy it as there are only a few left. Some customers start with an eight-year-old and move up to a twelve-year-old. 'Tis better if they start younger and move on. Many also come here for the beers because we are well known for being a very good Guinness house so customers would drink whiskey alongside their beers. People love the scent firstly. They then look at how it behaves in the glass, holding it to the light before sipping it slowly. Most people drink it without adding anything but it is recommended that a little water enhances the flavour.'

Margaret tells me about the tourist trade and her unofficial guiding role. 'I like the customer to be satisfied and try to direct them to some of our sites so my modus operandi is to make them happy. We have many countries represented here and all sorts of people. In 2009 Steven Spielberg was in the Burren for a week and came in every night. He was staying with the writer and poet David Whyte, who was holding a retreat with music, poetry and dance. Spielberg was here with his wife Kate Capshaw, their daughter and son-in-law. I got a signed photograph of him and he was a very personable man but of course we just treated him like every other customer. He drank Guinness and later told David that this was his favourite pub in the whole world.'

Ó Loclainn's features in many guidebooks and is on a celebrated Irish whiskey trail. Scrupulously clean and well run, its strength lies in its simplicity and in the absence of TV screens. At the bewitching hour there is barely elbow room in the main bar and in the words of one woman 'the only seats left are the toilet seats'. The back rooms are packed with drinkers propping up the walls and chatting animatedly. A group has gathered around a guitarist called Christine in a small snug. They applaud as she gently and tenderly strum-sings the landscape to life. 'The Mountains of Mourne', 'Carrickfergus', 'Galway Bay', 'The Fields of Athenry' and 'The Rocky Road to Dublin' are all part of the rich topographical musical tour that has visitors poring over their maps in search of the locations.

Many locals, including three men wearing blue Tour de Burren T-shirts, mingle alongside the polyglot clientele. The man from Thailand, who had been busy taking photographs of mirrors from long-forgotten distilleries, joins me just before closing time for the clinking of whiskey tumblers in a joint Black Bush nightcap where *sláinte* meets *chok-dee* in celebration of nutty sweetness. Wrinkling his nose above the glass, he raises an approving eyebrow and little finger in unison. I talk nonsensically to him about the 'drama of the attack' of certain *uisce beatha* and about my travels through an intoxicated landscape. He tells me about Chiang Mai where he used to live and where one day he hopes to return. With a farewell handshake, a 'velly nice to meet you Mister Paul', and a wave to 'Misses Margaret' now deep in a cartographic discussion with two Italians about the wonders of the Black Head coast road, he closes the door on one of the Burren's most sensory delights and on a bar reeking of a rapturous combination of whiskey and history.

Facing page Margaret Ó Loclainn, owner of Ó Loclainn's bar, Ballyvaughan
© Trevor Ferris

6

The Hypnotic Fascination of Mullaghmore

There are a handful of mountains and mountain landscapes
to which I return addictively like an unrequited lover craving
favours, secrets, intimacies.

Jim Crumley, *Among Mountains*

In the Irish mountain world it does not have superstar status.
It rarely merits a mention in the plethora of walking guides to
the hills of Ireland. On some maps it is not even shown. Many
people who set out to walk it have trouble finding it and often
lose themselves in the track of boreens that lead to this secluded
place. At a mere 191m it is one of the Burren's smaller hills. It
is not majestic, aristocratic, or anywhere near jaw-dropping. It
is not on most climbers' list since there is no serious challenge
in reaching the top. They scoff at the idea of it as a mountain.
It is too tame. No survival skills are required on this hillside – it
will take an hour or two at most to walk to the summit. And

yet, sitting in the extreme southeast of the accepted territory of the Burren almost falling off the edge, the hill of Mullaghmore, through a strange magnetism, encapsulates the heartbeat of the place.

Early one Easter Monday I tackled it again. I have been here in fifteen seasons. I have seen it in short days of mid-winter clarity, shimmering in a hazy summer heatwave, glowing in autumnal mist, and on dank days with skies of blanket greyness. By now its gentle inclines have a comforting familiarity, but each time the re-connection with the drama of it is stronger. There is a compelling softness about dawn. Early rising has been a feature of my life as a journalist working shifts in a newsroom. In a city certain things happen at dawn which only early risers see: pigeons picking through the vomit deposited by the night-before revellers, broken bottles and twisted beer cans filling the gutters, pavements littered with cigarette butts and, just occasionally, a blood red sunrise.

On this crisp morning Mullaghmore looks well-defined, revealing its folds and crannies. If it had an anthropomorphic personality, it would beam out a radiant smile greeting visitors with its stepped terraces and calling them in with a warming welcome. The difference with this early morning arousal is that the pavements are limestone and are littered with orchids, mountain avens, bird's-foot trefoil and shrubby cinquefoil. I register the presence in the distance of a vocal cuckoo, the spring leitmotif of the Burren: four vociferous calls at evenly spaced intervals.

Leaving the rhythm of the tarred road after a short distance, I step through a gap in a stone wall on to grey, thick-bedded limestone clints. Early purple orchids stand in solitary splendour alongside thorn bushes as I make my way to the foothills, passing the shores of Lough Gealáin which is part-turlough with changing levels through the seasons. The atmospheric fragility, the still air and the extended silences are apparent. This landscape is classic Burren. It requires careful stepping to avoid falling into the hollows and grykes or slipping on the clints, mindful that they may tilt, and working my way round enormous boulders. Wrong-footing yourself is an occupational walking hazard here and requires attention as to where you put your feet. I enjoy the scenery on walks but here it is a case of eyes on the ground until I gain some height. Stopping to check my flora book, I catch sight of a frog lurking inconspicuously in a gryke. I watch its erratic hopping progress. It pauses for a few seconds, jumping from clint to clint, before making the big leap into a small oval-shaped pool of shallow water. Basking contentedly in the sun, it ignores my presence and then, without as much as a humble croak or chirp, disappears swiftly into a green fern-filled world.

My *AA Illustrated Guide to Ireland* describes Mullaghmore as having 'a high rock strata, folded and contorted like dough'. Tim Robinson says its 'terraced sides are so curved as to make it look like a layer-cake that has sunk in the cooking'. From the lower slopes of the terrace, I pick up a grassy track for ten minutes. It feels much easier on my feet and a contrast from the dull thud and 'clunk-clunk' of the clints. I admire a trio of potato-shaped erratics and clamber over another wall, my third en route to the summit. Carpets of geraniums – up to thirty in each clump – are spread out before me. I come to a sheer 12-metre-high cliff face and survey the sweep of the countryside. As daylight strengthens, Mullaghmore works its magic. With its foothills and terraces, it is a haunting place of peace. A shout here could travel 160km perhaps landing somewhere in west Wicklow. The noises that I note are an unseen aircraft, and the throbbing of a reversing tractor. I negotiate three tiers of terracing which involves some scrambling to reach the top.

The combination of sun and walking has brought perspiration beads and I pause to remove my fleece. On the

Glacial erratic at Black Head with facial expression
similar to an Easter Island stone statue © Marty Johnston

Above: Winter scene along the coast road near Ballyvaughan © Trevor Ferris

Facing page, top: Stonewall, Rock Forest near Mullaghmore © Trevor Ferris

Facing page, bottom: Bloody cranesbill, one of the spring specialties of the Burren flora © Marty Johnston

Rare black swans with mute swan, Lough Murri © Trevor Ferris

second terracing, before tackling another set of stepped stones, I watch the clouds move lower. The higher orchids have a much more withered appearance and look past their best. I make my way up another cliff-side and across a short plateau to the final terracing – this one marked with scree to the top where a chest-high cairn denotes the summit. Someone has placed six flat stones on top of each other, with a couple of smaller ones on top. I place my own.

I feel my heart beating strongly, not because of the climb, but because of a heightened sense that I am alone, out of reach of other humans, sharply aware of being alive. Quietly I draw breath at the top, reflecting on the silence. There is no trace, sight or sound of the three Cs: cars, cows and chainsaws. Over my left ear another double C – *Cuculus canorus* – again looks for my attention.

I pull off my rucksack, drink a quarter of my litre bottle of water in one gulp and enjoy a lunch in the company of banded snails sleeping on the grass and rocks. As I munch my way through a fat brie and bacon sandwich, I count ten snails surrounding my boots. Some flies hover, attracted by the smell of my soup, but quickly disappear. Several wasps fidget, and bees cruise by. There is no wind. A spider dances over my map that is lying open on the grass beside me. A fly lands on Kilnaboy.

Moving from the microscopic to the macroscopic, I use my binoculars to pick up the cardinal directions of widescreen Burren. The summit of Mullaghmore offers a new perspective of the landmass and distances, a place to grasp the dimensions and provide broad vistas to all points of the compass. To my immediate north lies the main Burren territory. Dozens of mighty boulders are strewn at intervals across the limestone. A long procession of sun-wakened hills sits in a restful line of neatly spaced intervals: Knockanes, Turloughmore and off to the northwest Slievecarran. Immediately to the west lies Glasgeivnagh

Hill, while on the south side, unassuming green fields fill the picture. I pick out isolated bungalows, a red barn, and an old square farmhouse with smoke belching from its chimney. A long line of trees stretching for several kilometres delimits the Burren's natural southern boundary. Faraway, heavily pregnant clouds hang over the hills of south Clare. Fields of cattle sit in the sun. A pair of ravens glides across my view, shouting incomprehensible phrases before crashing with a distinct lack of finesse on to the limestone. Beyond the main road to the south and east are a series of long, thin, quaintly named, freshwater loughs – Inchiquin, Atedaun, Cullaun, George, Ballyeighter and Bunny. These lakes, just outside the barony of the Burren, are all-year-round loughs in that they retain their water throughout the summer and winter, unlike turloughs.

Eastwards the limestone continues for a few kilometres before giving way to a technicolor landscape of vegetation, forests and fields with farms and outbuildings. Half-a-dozen rectangular lakes sit undisturbed with trees reflected in the water. Small settlements are visible leading to Gort. In the far distance, the Slieve Aughty Mountains, a long, low range of hills, mark the limit of visibility. I count eight windmills on the western section. Thankfully, these blights on the countryside have not protruded this far. Westwards the clouds turn dark. A long, high ridge blocks any view beyond to the sea or the western side of the Burren. The ridge is a mixture of rock and green fields divided by hedges and trees. Every hundred metres or so, a farmhouse or bungalow sits in alignment to the road. Cattle and sheep mingle sharing the grass below the cliff face. An orange tractor idles at a farm building, the only sign of life I have seen from the summit. Mullaghmore and the area immediately surrounding it represent the Burren in miniature. Lough Gealáin is a ring of bright water. It is a lake or turlough that performs conjuring tricks: now you see it, now you don't – although not quite at such high speed.

These self-contained ephemeral turloughs dry up in the summer and fill again in the winter.

I often amuse myself on mountaintops by noting what is not here – what the eye cannot see. Missing from the landscape in this case are energetic mountain streams, cascading waterfalls, TV and phone masts, electricity pylons, very little noise-making activity, and the human voice. Occasionally, on these moments, I indulge myself, reflecting on the inner silence: a time and a place to be rid of personal problems, of heavy burdens and anxieties; a place to see the light, shapes, and textures of the landscape in all their infinite variety. If Mullaghmore is the Ayers Rock of Ireland, then it is a good place to experience the Dream Time like the Aboriginal people in Australia. Like them, I too believe in the power of dreams which is why I keep a dream journal by my bedside and handy for a mountaintop siesta. Edward Abbey tells us that in the Dream Time the wise old men of the outback say we made our beginning, from the Dream Time we come, and into the Dream Time, after death, we shall return.

Mullaghmore is a place where you are alone with your thoughts . . . or at least where I thought I was. Out of the corner of my eye I feel a watching presence, glimpse a movement and hear a gentle rustle. Over my right shoulder, a party of eight feral goats, including a kid with white shaggy hair, has arrived unobtrusively 50m from me. Gathered in silent colloquia, they stare at me intently with profound and attentive watchfulness. I stare back. They have come to inquire as to my place on their land. They stare at each other before contemplating me again with an indignant yet vigilant look. The glaring contest lasts for five minutes. They seem a bit stand-offish. I feel they are looking down their large noses at me, uncertain of this intruder in their midst. Several have long unkempt beards. Three are brown and white, three are milk chocolate and two are milk-white, one with a black beard. Like Ted Hughes' horses, they stand 'megalith-still'. Suddenly one with a pure white coat breaks this peaceful tableau vivant, lifts its leg and comically scratches an ear. I imagine they do not perceive me as any threat, nor are they going to attack me, but they do not appear to want to come closer. They seem to have taken mild umbrage that I have invaded their high territory. I feel a slight sense of unease at being watched but gradually warm to their presence. Being born under the sign of Capricorn, I have always had an admiration for goats. I unzip the side pocket of my rucksack and take out my leather hip flask. The sun temporarily pokes its way through clouds. Silently, I sip my Burren 'tea', offering a quiet toast to my ear-scratching four-legged friends: here's lookin' at you, kids.

Behind the façade of serenity, Mullaghmore has had a troubled recent history. How different it might all have been. A proposal, regarded by many as outrageous, to build an interpretative centre at the base of the mountain caused a ten-year debate in the 1990s, generating thousands of words of heated argument. It was an emotionally divisive battle unleashing passionate protest voices, arousing controversy and stirring enflamed feelings. It stimulated writers, poets and musicians into creative action, angered environmentalists, and served as a wake-up call to those who care about the landscape on their doorstep. But not everyone was against the development and there was considerable local support for it on the strength of job-creation and the amount of revenue it would generate for the local economy. In a colourful quote, a local councillor described the opposition to the centre as 'blow-ins, hippies, homosexuals, drug smokers, intellectuals and non meat-eaters'. After a long, vigorous and expensive campaign by the Burren Action Group the plan was finally seen off in the spring of 2000. By that stage excavations and preparations were already under way for a car park.

Looking across the calcified landscape unsullied by human

activity, I reflect on the desecration that has taken place and how it might appear to a futurologist if the developers had their way. Spooling forward to the 2050s, I imagine that if the interpretative centre had been built, by this stage it would have reached spoilation level: the visionary splendour of the place is no more. By mid-twenty-first century the uglification of this one-time sacred precinct is complete. Flights land with regularity at Mullaghmore International Airport depositing sightseers and trippers. The clamour of thousands of visitors each week bring an assortment of litter, noise pollution, fumes from traffic and buildings, the whole visual wear and tear, including the impact of people scrambling over the fragile walls, tramping on the flowers and showing complete disregard for the environment. On a busy week in summer more than 50,000 people are to be found here.

Traffic is queuing to fill the car parks with a maelstrom of tour coaches, minibuses, RVs, 4WDs, land cruisers, super-jeeps with 64-inch tyres, motor homes and the most hateful of all these contraptions, the so-called 'mega-people carriers'. Consider the length of the human congas for the toilet blocks, tearooms and audiovisual presentations. All the things people go into the hills to escape from are gone, the magic destroyed. By now it is a wounded and damaged landscape, lacerated and stained with the blotches of visitors and their cars, contaminated with their collective detritus and, worst of all, their noise footprint. I am thankful that I brought my ear defenders along with me to celebrate my nonagenarian years. Small parties sit at tables in the blinding March sunshine outside the newly opened Limestone Pavement Bar where a group of three musicians is entertaining the crowds. Two rival hotels have sprouted up and are fully booked each weekend throughout the summer. Large signposts point the visitor in the direction of 'Mullaghmore: The Mysterious Wonder Walk Path'. It is just one of a network of man-made walkways that in some cases involved tearing up or obscuring sections of precious pavement. We have spoiled the place we love.

On top of all this, climate change has had a big bearing on how the Burren looks more than forty years on with spring starting in mid-January. The Burren spring conference is held in December and the annual Burren in Bloom festival, which we recall took place throughout May, has been brought forward to February. Although most flowers have endured and the tough mountain avens, gentians and orchids continue to flourish in large numbers (the early purple orchids now bloom in December), some plants and trees are having trouble adapting to the rising temperatures and there is an alarming threat of extinctions. Untroubled by the earth's warming, the glacial erratics are holding firm while the karst has not altered fundamentally although the continuing encroachment of hazel has penetrated into many more areas.

Fields that in the early part of the twenty-first century were bright green are now parched brown, the result of hotter springs and summers in the intervening four decades. It is still a place of paradoxes. Rainfall has increased dramatically leading to the limestone dissolving in areas that were much admired by visitors back in 2010. But against this, the Caher River, the only overground river in the Burren, has completely dried out and followed the example of the summer turloughs. Sea surface temperatures have risen dramatically each decade since the turn of the century and the waves at the famed surfing spot near the Cliffs of Moher have more than trebled in size.

Thankfully the concertina is still an essential part of Clare's social fabric and the musical climate is as powerful as ever. The new foot-tapping songs from the three-man group sitting outside the bar include 'Forty Shades of Beige', 'The Wearin' o' the Brown' and 'Four Sunburnt Fields'.

This fleeting glimpse of the future may sound impossibly

gloomy, botanically unlikely and musically improbable. Although I have taken a fanciful leap into the future, some of it is based on scientific speculation in a report in 2008 entitled 'Changing Shades of Green' produced by the Irish American Climate Project. The main findings of the report on how climate change will affect Ireland predict large differences in rainfall: up to 12 per cent more during the winters and up to 12 per cent less in the summers, as well as more frequent bog bursts and the loss of the potato as an important commercial crop because of harsh droughts.

Environmental and cultural changes of the future remain the realm of crystal ball gazers and no one can say with any degree of certainty exactly how Ireland or the Burren will look by the 2050s. The report is loaded with a number of shallow, speculative phrases couched in terms such as 'could be', 'may be' and 'remains to be seen'. Who can possibly predict what oil resources will be like, whether we will be driving vehicles at all, or if we will have used up so much that we have come full circle and returned again to a simple, eco-friendly, pastoral people walking, cycling and dancing at the crossroads.

To come back to the present, ironically the very act of driving to visit a precious landscape contributes to its degradation. It is true to say there is a contradiction because I arrived and will leave by car. Meekly, in my defence, I can only quote Walt Whitman:

> Do I contradict myself?
> Very well then I contradict myself
> I am large, I contain multitudes.

I have come alone with only the wind and birds for company, and will respect what is here. My point is if you multiply one vehicle one thousandfold, or even one hundredfold, you are left with the following audio: engines thrumming, doors slamming, exhausts revving, horns honking, radios blaring, and the general stench and brouhaha of families, holidaymakers, and thousands of daytrippers (mostly tripping over the clints). The nuances of the landscape, the mood of the place, and the atmosphere mean little to them. Coach tours and mountains do not go together. They are an unhappy juxtaposition. They have different priorities. As bedfellows, they are not just strange, they are manifestly incompatible. Had this development gone ahead, there would have been no aural contest between the collision of the sounds of human technology and the sounds of nature.

Another issue surrounding the controversy over the interpretative centre related to the quality of life of local people, brought about by the pressure on roads that were not built to cope with high volumes of traffic. The saga raised questions about why a silvery-grey stony place needs interpretation, or, as one local referred to it, an 'interruptive' centre. Undoubtedly there is much to understand, but why spoil, or indeed 'interrupt' the very life of the place that you are trying to understand by building on it?

I watch the shadow of a passing cloud. A flash of sunlight clears the air. With its protracted and vigorous singing, a long-winded skylark brings me back to the present. The bird is hard to see but not hard to hear. Its song reverberates across the hilltop, a delectable sound of Mullaghmore. This reinforces the notion that the key to the mountain is solitude and silence. As a landscape empty of people, it affords peace of mind. It offers a place where you can come to an appreciation of the scope and scale of the scenery, feel alone, withdraw from the crowds, and where the only voice is the voice of the landscape as you indulge in some mental futuristic free-floating.

The nature writer Michael Viney says of Mullaghmore: 'No amount of knowledge about its origins in geology and Neolithic overgrazing can diminish its rapt, aboriginal power: it is the Ayers

Rock of Ireland, if yet without the tourists clambering over it.' I have always admired his description of Mullaghmore as 'an Earth-object of almost hypnotic fascination'. The prosaic meaning of Mullaghmore, or in Irish *Mullach Mór*, is 'great summit'. The theologian, philosopher and author John O'Donohue, who died in 2008, summed up in a poem its greatness for him:

> Mullaghmore Mountain is the tabernacle of the Burren, its folded shape evokes a poignancy and a sense of reverence. Once glimpsed it can never be forgotten. The history and the mystery of the Burren come alive in its elegance and silence.

To the superficial observer, Mullaghmore, like the wider Burren, at first looks drab and featureless. There may appear little that is particularly special about the area. It is not a holy mountain in

Mullaghmore Mountain © Marty Johnston

the vein of Croagh Patrick, 112km to the north with its human motorway to the summit. Mercifully 30,000 people are not to be found climbing it on the last Sunday of July. You come here to take the pulse of the place and feel small in surroundings that are not enormous, but where the sounds that are here are magnified. A place of austere beauty with a strange and compelling power, it is a lodestone – a limestone lodestone – of the highest order by which all is measured; it is a precious place where, after each peregrination, I feel re-energised, uplifted, cleansed and where, to invoke Uncle Walt again, without competition from others, 'I sound my barbaric yawp over the roofs of the world.'

7

Time and Tide

Bloody-minded sort of place, it looks,
Where old faiths shrivel, old names are defaced.
But out of these barren flags, this crazed landscape,
Jut the resilient heads of a melting-pot
Of flowers from the high and cold, the low and hot,
The wet, wet places. All at ease on this rockface.

Like finding love in someone disliked at first.

U. A. Fanthorpe, 'The Burren'

A diaphanous aura of faint shifting light plays over the soft air of the Burren hills. The ethereal quality of the light often has a bearing on the colours. There are times when the limestone twinkles and scintillates with a shimmering effect across this mellow landscape. When the sun's rays catch the summit of Cappanawalla it can reactivate it and look as though a flashlight is shining on it.

Ceaselessly, the light and the limestone play tricks on the eyes; they dazzle, sparkle and glitter on bright days. At other times the light soaks into a pale wash, merging sky and earth. Beams of bright sun pierce through the sky, spotlighting fields, walls and small enclaves of limestone. The sun, with its repeated appearances and disappearances, acts as a scene-changer. Chameleon-like, the limestone scene-shifts at the whim of the light and the weather – at once an ochreous pink, an hour later with grey and white hues, sections of hills are plunged into darkness; later a tint of purple and after another hour, a dappled sky.

Crisp light on an invigorating March or October morning has a confident feel revealing fine details. Winter light can be deceitful – or at least deceptive – enticing you outside when you suddenly feel the coolness of the air, although it is often compensated for by a rare calm. The low-angled morning sunlight causes the fields to occasionally flash bright white in their winter garb.

There is a dour unforgiving about the Burren at the start of the year. On a bone-chilling January day with a raw wind it can seem a place of blackness where daylight lingers for only a few hours. The tourists have disappeared but the sound of the birds has not diminished. One St Brigid's Day (1 February) I watched a low, muffled sun – lacking in apricity – peep from behind clouds casting a long, glossy, black sheen over the pavement, walls, erratics and stones at Murroughtoohy South along the coast road. It had a dreary countenance yet there was an earthiness to it – a black-brown feel as an outburst of rain suddenly returned, then just as quickly cleared leaving a subdued mood. The wintry showers, accompanied by a concoction of snow, sleet and hail, were punctuated by brief glimpses of rainbow slashes adorning the sky – far from dazzling but still enough to gladden a cold winter's heart and break the sullen atmosphere. My car clock timed the setting sun at 5.41 p.m.

As darkness falls I walk across clumps of grass that in a few months' time will be a riot of colours. Lurking around in the murk I look into small circular kamenitzas filled with water and find they are hardened to a consistency similar to that of crème brûlée. Delicately I tiptoe over them. With boyish curiosity I dip the top of my boot into one and shatter what turns out to be surprisingly thick ice with thin stalks of grass embedded in it. The sharp ice feels good to touch. Clumps of grass are talced with a light ground frost. I lift a large chunk then drop it on the pavement shattering the shards into small fragments.

In my short, crunching stroll through grass I watch an active gang of hooded crows. Pied wagtails flit busily around, and glossy, black-capped bullfinches hop from wall to boulder and on to the limestone. From the branch of a bare and burnished hawthorn tree a solitary robin sings its heart out, its throat trembling with the cold. Back in town a hardened frost with a sharp sting – a rare occurrence here – sets in as car windscreens freeze over.

The gradations of light of different times of the day carry their own weight. Golden shafts of morning light at Corcomroe Abbey lend it a special magic. Equally beguiling is to see Gragan East shrouded with a swirling chiffon of mist drifting through the valley. Midday light can be sparkling on a bright day while late-afternoon light picks up different textures. Some nights the deepening hues mean that there is no perceptible horizon. The Atlantic and the sky blend into a seamless, hazy void, occasionally the one being a mirror image of the other. Water and sky meld and it becomes impossible to distinguish the boundary between the two. There is a feeling of unbounded space. The horizon is lost. The French call this time *entre chien et lupe* (between the dog and the wolf). It is a period that feels both tranquil and threatening.

Twilight has powerful transformational quality. The 'violet hour' of T. S. Eliot can bring with it a fretwork of shadows with a before and after feel. With the slow disappearance of the sun, a sadness hovers in the air at this special transition time. The light of the sinking sun travels through the atmosphere catching dust, gases and liquids floating around. On a clear night an afterglow with a tantalising resonance is visible around Black Head. Watching the darkness slowly unfold in late evening is to see the Burren at its most captivating. It is a soft translucent light. For photographers this is the time to capture Cartier-Bresson's 'decisive moment' – which may last only a few minutes before the final fiery curtain call but is a divine moment.

Often I watch the light travel across the terracing so that some parts are spotlit and others remain in shadow – a contest of illumination between those that have the pleasure of sunbathing in slivers of golden light and those that have not. The moon re-enchants the surroundings too. The multicoloured spectacle of a corona around it is best seen when the moon reaches perigee, its closest distance to the earth for the lunar month. The coloured rings around the moon are a faint blue towards the inside and brown on the outside.

The Atlantic is a huge pond, its surface only occasionally ruffled on a calm night by a gentle wind or the puttering of a fishing boat. Slowly, it conceals and reveals itself as the light plays a game with the ocean. But sometimes changes occur at breakneck speed and the raking light glances across the limestone. The eye dances around the place, ricocheting from the light coming off the erratics, bouncing along the sharply defined hills and walls, to the carpet of mountain avens, and down to the sea. A skittish shower often arrives, washing the limestone, leaving a glitter effect after which the colours take on a new intensity in the clear light. The rain rinses it clean, adding a glaze. Trees have a newly showered look about them, the clints glisten as though hosed down, polished to a military shine, droplets drip from the tiny flowers, and the tarmac takes on a pristine sheen as the sun steams the remains of the surface water off the road. Heavy rain disappears rapidly through the fissures. At other times you may find yourself caught in a prodigious downpour as water slides off every stone and leaf.

The weather's drift is seen at its best here. As befits a west of Ireland county, Clare's weather performance can be notoriously fickle. A Burren hailstorm can be exhilarating, disturbing and very wet. A peel of thunder in the distance is followed by a crack of lightning. The energy of the rain is powerful. It falls in huge drops, attacking you suddenly and quickly diluting the scene to misty gauze. There are few better places to appreciate the shifting dynamism in nature.

The rain hurtles in off the sea in vehement bursts but most of the time it is softer. I have experienced days when it is as light as talcum powder while other times I have raced for cover from the pounding hailstones. The energy of the rain can intensify the nature of things. The limestone is invigorated by continuous sheets of rain drumming on it filling every depression with puddles. Hares and birds take shelter. A typical day often will consist of a succession of showers, sunshine and rainbows bathing the landscape in light. Some locals like to refer to it by a musical analogy: Vivaldi weather – four seasons in one day.

~~~

'Do you think it'll thunder?' a rosy-glowed farmer with a lopsided, teeth-stained smile once asked me during a mid-morning stroll along a marshy lane. Leaning over a five-bar steel gate, he sniffed the weather and surveyed the dark inland sky, a spectacular sight often occurring in the morning with anvil tops to the clouds. Later that afternoon the sky had cleared and the day's drama was complete with the eventual arrival of thunderstorms but no lightning.

The walls may form the backbone to the landscape but the sky as a source of light is the backcloth. It is a place of dramatic and restless skies; this chiaroscuro is best appreciated from the top of Cappanawalla or Abbey Hill. There are times when the sky seems to go upwards forever, working a sorcerer's repertoire of iridescent lighting tricks.

Visitors often remark on the beauty and colour of the clouds that overhang the Burren. With their exquisite hues, the infinite diurnal variations of clouds know no bounds: white fluffy cotton wool, grey blending with the limestone so you cannot see the grykes in the sky where they separate; clouds, white as chalk, scud at speed on occasion, their shadow cast large across the terracing. On other days a flurry of milky white broccoli-shaped ones line up in geometrically arranged banks. Then there are the days of bleached-out white or etiolated clouds; days when the clouds seems positively light-hearted curling thinly in a wispy blue sky; days of a cloud-veiled sky; days of skeins of, in meteorologists' parlance, silver altocumulus, when the small, rounded clouds look like the woolly backs of sheep and you get the sense that rain will soon be on the way. There are thin skimmed-milk days when rays of sunlight shine through, closely followed by days when no clouds slide across the sky and it is an anaemic mass, pale and listless.

When the dull weather snuffs all colour from the landscape a blanket of amorphous cloud covers the sky. This is the brooding, featureless, deep mid-winter sky. On these overcast stratiform days clouds develop ragged lumps of grey with a lack of sunshine and rain falls for a long time. Sometimes clouds dangle low, hanging over the hills so that you imagine if you were on top of one you could almost reach out and feel their whiteness. On days of a high skyline, or days of a sombre rain-filled sky you are uncertain what clothes to wear. You bring waterproofs just in case and within half-an-hour the sun has come out, closely followed by a cloudburst. On one mind-numbingly cold winter's morning I set out on a walk well prepared for the weather and ended up shedding most of what I had brought.

The number of clouds flaunting themselves in the sky varies considerably. On occasion they hover only over the land but not over the sea. The reverse is sometimes the case. On drifting cloud days, they deliver an inland shadow over Slievecarran; other days, vertical clouds race across the landscape. Rarely, though, do the shadows race – generally they move sedately, almost imperceptibly, with celestial scene-shifting.

Meteorologists have identified at least thirty categories of cloud structure ranging from stratus (near the ground) through altocumulus (medium level) right up to the towering high cirrus clouds (up to 8km above our heads). Whatever you demand, in terms of size, silhouettes, spectres and suggestions the Clare clouds offer it, providing an essential element in the Burren atmosphere: clouds cherubic, clouds magnificent, clouds exciting, clouds glamorous, clouds unobtrusive, clouds benign, clouds spindly, clouds gigantic, clouds enigmatic, clouds delicate, clouds imperious, forlorn clouds, feathery clouds, menacing clouds, windswept clouds, clouds with cauliflower heads, clouds with long tails, clouds with anvil shapes, and super clouds heaped high in the sky. In short, enough clouds to keep a nephologist happy for a lifetime. With darkness descending the pink blush of a sky behind Abbey and Turlough Hills enlivens a dusk drive to New Quay. There is a special resonance in the pageant of the evening sky when the combination of light, sea and limestone produces a golden lustre.

Once on a late May evening as I stepped carefully over freshly washed limestone at Sheshymore, I looked up to see a pair of rainbows – known to meteorologists as a supernumerary – created by light interfering with itself in the raindrops. After the heavy showers had ended the first bow was vivid with a solid arc of intense colours; the second lay just above the main one, much fainter than its twin and with its spectrum of colours reversed.

~~~

When you have had your fill of clouds, flowers, stones and archaeological remains it is pleasurable, over a coffee, to indulge in a favourite pastime: anthropological fieldwork, otherwise known as people-watching. One of the appeals of this laid-back place is to slip down a gear, reverse a decade or two and succumb to idleness. Dawdling in the sunshine outside a cafe with a large latte one spring morning, I watched the workaday rhythms of the ordinary daily life in 'Dallyvaughan' (as it is sometimes known) where everyone seems to know everyone.

The village is being tarted up for the summer tourist invasion. Dustsheets, the colour of a straw boater, litter the pavements. Three separate teams of painters and decorators are taking advantage of the sunny May morning. At a rhythmic pace, harvest green is rolled on to the walls of Logue's Lodge by a navy-overalled man standing on the fifth rung of a wooden ladder. A younger man, with a green baseball cap with the word 'Ellesse' on it, applies a black weather shield to the window frames. Every fifteen minutes they slide steel stepladders along the pavement. The older man sips water from a large brown mug with a broken handle.

Two doors down at Quinn's gift shop a thin man on wooden stepladders puts the finishing touches of gloss to the black frames around a large plate glass window. At the corner two denim-clad men, halfway up a long metal ladder, pebble-dash with a cream weather cladding the upper-storey of Hyland's Burren Hotel which fronts on to the main road and is the nerve-centre of Ballyvaughan. The village slumbers in the peace of a painterly morning. No one seems in any particular hurry to go anywhere or do anything. At Logue's, every few minutes, the gaffer in overalls greets the passers-by with a friendly hello. They step on the road rather than walk under his ladders or trample his dustsheets. He seems to know the whole village.

'Howiya Jimmy.'

'Only middlin', that's a grand day.'

'Howiya Packie.'

'Ach hangin' together like a pair of trousers.'

'Howiya Sheila.'

'Isn't it great to see men at work on a grand mornin' like that.'

Often delivered with an emphatic force, the 'Howiyas' do not come with the intonation of a question mark, more a genial enquiry about life in general. Friendly greetings always amuse me and set me thinking. When someone asks 'how are you?' rarely do people's answers contain a detailed medical bulletin; seldom do they even complain about anything. There is usually an inane reply to what, in the first place, is a rhetorical question. As I nurse a latte refill, and keep an eye on the painters, I think of smart-alec answers that I can recall to the eternal question, 'How are you?'

I always loved Roger McGough's line from his poem 'Bits of Me':

When people ask: 'How are you?'
I say, 'Bits of me are fine.'

When Laurie Lee was asked how he was, he replied: 'I'm still a going concern, but a bit concerned about my going.'

In Picasso's case he was usually to be found: 'In a state of disconcerted anguish.'

The journalist John Diamond's rejoinder to the query was:

'I'm okay I suppose, within the usual existential constraints.'

In Douglas Adams' book, *The Hitchhiker's Guide to the Galaxy*, the earthling, Arthur Dent's response to 'How are you?' is one of the genre's best: 'Like a military academy – bits of me keep passing out.'

Henry David Thoreau's profound, yet instantly recognisable reply to the 'Howiya Henry?' question, invariably was: 'I'm leading a life of quiet desperation.'

And the journalist Tiziano Terzani's reply to 'How are you?' was: 'I am very well; it's just my body that is rotting and I am going to leave it behind.'

My mind-wandering musings end when the Bus Éireann service from Galway pulls up tailed by a string of camper vans and caravanettes. A German couple and two young women disembark from the bus. I wander around lest anyone dare ask about my health, state of mind or general well-being. Ballyvaughan has not changed much over the years. There is disagreement over the spelling of its name. Signposts opt for Ballyvaghan, without the u, others insist on the u; some call it simply Ballyvee which gets round the problem. The village is a hotbed of signs, ranking as the signpost capital of Ireland. But despite a large one at the T-junction tourists still have trouble finding their way and on my visits I am constantly being asked for the road to Doolin or Black Head. There is often a bustle about the place – never too crowded but just an agreeable number of visitors. It has three cafes, three gift shops, four pubs, a supermarket, visitor centre, launderette, hairdresser, post office, a church, two hotels, several B&Bs, a primary school, a small enterprise centre, a health centre, and restaurateurs who like to rename their premises every so often to reflect culinary changes.

It is an instantly likeable village where there is delightfully little to do. Sometimes it can seem almost out-of-time, like a place steeped in a distant and innocent decade such as 1950s' Ireland. Off season I have found a serenity that almost touches melancholy. Perhaps Ballyvaughan is best described in terms of what it does not have. Far from the surfing crowds, it has no youth hostel, no caravan sites on the edge of the village, no neon lighting, no traffic lights, no parking meters, no billboards, no bookies, and not even an ATM to be plundered or rammed. The Burren has never managed to entice a bank to set up shop in any of its villages, nor indeed insert a hole in the wall. You may, as you make your way around the twisty roads, encounter the navy blue north Clare mobile Ulster Bank van (open Thursday from 11.20 a.m. to 12.10 p.m. in Ballyvaughan). It is an important part of many people's weekly routine and one of the few areas of Ireland where a mobile bank still visits. The Burren is protected from those in a hurry by a paucity of transport links. No trains service the area and a limited bus service links it to Galway and smaller towns. Although there is no picture-house, a 100-seater mobile cinema, Cinemobile – Ireland's only cinema on wheels – visits Ballyvaughan from time to time, setting up in the national school car park.

There is also no crime, or at least, in my experience, very little. I once left a shoulder bag with money, credit cards and mobile phone in a bird hide and, an hour later when I realised I had left it behind, went back to retrieve it but discovered it had gone. Minor panic set it. I cancelled my credit cards, told the hotel about my loss and attempted to contact the police. The staff told me not to worry – that it would be handed in.

'People here wouldn't keep that,' said Carmel, the receptionist. 'I'm pretty sure it'll be returned by this afternoon.' In the meantime she suggested, in case it was handed in, we should report it missing to the Garda in the station. We tried phoning, twice – no answer. Then, it dawned on her: 'It's Thursday, his day off – he doesn't come in on a Thursday.'

109

Later that same day a local woman who had found my possessions in the hide and taken them for safe-keeping, tracked me down via the local grapevine and handed them over to me.

Few developments blight the Burren. Apart from small clusters of holiday homes and thatched cottages, it has not reached the epidemic proportions of the bungalow blitz that afflicts large parts of Donegal or Achill Island. Thankfully there are few signs or symbols of gentrification. Its location is its strength. Four or five roads and tracks on its periphery lead down to the sea; quiet culs-de-sac that come to an abrupt end where they meet the Atlantic unsignposted and unknown to strangers. All this means that opportunities for building are limited and the developers are forced to move on elsewhere leaving the Burren largely undesecrated.

~~~

'Don't hurry yourself,' says the woman in the cafe. 'Finish your coffee, there's no rush.'

Rivulets of rain snake slowly down the window as I stretch my refill to last until the weather improves. Time passes. Chairs are stacked on tables, floors brushed, money counted, and blinds drawn. It has just gone five o'clock. Another day's trading is coming to an end but in the Tea Junction cafe they have all the time in the world to shut up shop. An aroma of strong brewing coffee hangs in the air.

The only other customers, two women in their forties, finish off a conversation about men – past and present – in their lives. One ends every sentence with a long sigh and a speech tag 'As you do' and the other rejoinders with a minimal encourager 'As if . . .' followed by an even heavier sigh. For thirty years, in the hurly-burly world of journalism I have been 'quick-coffeed' on numerous occasions in between rushing back with stories, meeting frantic deadlines, script-writing in a cameraman's car, or job-changing within the media. The new image of the first decade of the twenty-first century – 'a coffee to go' – is a culture largely alien to the Burren.

One of the aspects of the place that has always fascinated me is the easy-going nature of the way of life. The slow tempo of the Burren takes time to work on you. There is an uncrowded quietness. No one seems to be in any particular hurry; in fact, nothing must be done at speed since that would be hostile to the spirit of the place which has a sane disregard for haste. To say they have their own timescale and operate at their own relaxed pace is an understatement. Spend a few days here and you begin to realise the insignificance of time – watches and clocks seem irrelevant. Time is a loose concept and passes unnoticed. Perhaps more than anywhere else in Ireland, time here has enormous elasticity. Slowness gradually seeps into your bones.

A typical Burren day starts slowly. Often the mist, never in a rush to clear, lingers all morning or until around eleven o'clock – assuming you have still not lost track of time. Its eventual disappearance and the emergence of the slow-motion sun is a major contributory factor in the decision as to how to spend the rest of the day: on the hills, on the lower slopes of the terracing, walking the coast, a spot of bird-watching perhaps, observing the flickering wings of the Orange-Tip butterfly, or daydreaming in cafes while eavesdropping on conversations.

From my observations I have noticed many animals in a state of light catalepsy – the condition between numbness and lethargy. Burly cows chew slow cud then contentedly munch a mixed salad of tall orchids, grass and seaweed. They have a placid look, slouching as they roll their eyes and swing their heads and tails. Goats move sluggishly, if at all, while dozing geese languish on back roads. Standing stock-still with erect ears, the Burren's donkeys bring a smile and pop up in all sorts of unexpected places: a field at Rathborney, beside the bridge on the coast road in Ballyvaughan, and on the limestone at Murrough.

Can there be another village in Ireland that has such undemonstrative dogs and cats? The Ballyvaughan cats are alert but unperturbed about their next meal. Solitary ginger toms dart casually down alleyways and at night semi-invisible black prowlers slip around the edge of the village.

But the most admired cat is Mrs Puss who attracts an endless stream of curiosity from her position outside the Village Stores in Ballyvaughan. The cat's tortoiseshell colouring – a mottled pattern of black, orange, yellow and white – is part of the attraction for tourists and shoppers in need of stress relief. She looks as though she has just been through a heavyweight boxing bout and been inflicted with a nasty black eye. Motionless but with a high strokeability factor, the cat lies curled on a chair, sometimes preferring an unnoticed ground position in the corner.

Like most cats Mrs Puss snoozes a large part of her day away. She seems abnormally relaxed and unflinching at even the slightest touch or interest in her siesta. I have watched the reaction of both cat and customers, many of whom pet her as though a good luck charm. As an entry point for those beginning their Burren journey, she has developed a talismanic quality. After alighting at the bus stop beside the shop, visitors receive their befurred blessing. Tourists like to touch her while delivering a friendly greeting. Once, a Norwegian man, who did not notice her on the picnic table, almost dropped his hefty rucksack on her, just missing her head by a whisker or two; she did not bat a docile eyelid.

Cautiously, children approach, crouching down to stare and sometimes she responds with a half-open eye or a long slow wink. 'Is it a dog or a cat . . . is it real?' a young boy once enquired of his parents. He deliberated over whether or not to touch her, then gently stroked her and followed this with a firm yank of her soft furry tail and an even firmer rebuke from his father. Elderly women are often intrigued by her and, as a sidetrack from shopping, like to tickle under her chin as if a newborn baby. One woman sitting smoking at a table once told me that she 'just mugs' everyone who passes through. Frequently tourists drop grateful crumbs to her strategic position at one side of the picnic table although she does not seem to like Guinness cake. When she has had her fill of their leftovers she slinks around the side of the shop to her warm little shack at the back.

Mrs Puss is unconcerned by all the fuss. Nor does she appear interested in birds although Jim, the shop owner, describes her as a 'great ratter'. She seems to especially enjoy grooming and vigorous tugging of her fur as well as washing all over with her long tongue. In the morning, after a wash-and-brush-up, ears pricked, she is alert to the noisy comings and goings of delivery vans pulling up to restock the supermarket. She often scratches furiously, with her head jerking forward and gazing intently straight ahead with deadly concentration before feverishly slaughtering some flies.

The ultimate accolade came in 2009 when the cat's own Facebook page, the Ballyvaughan Tongue Cat Club, was set up by students. Quickly Mrs Puss built up a fan base with more than forty friends. Fussed over but unfazed by fame, Ballyvaughan's glamour puss is the Burren's most photographed tabby, the animal version of the Poulnabrone dolmen.

The most courteous dog to be seen in public is Trixie, the rheumy-eyed, black-and-white collie occupying the doormat outside O'Donoghue's pub along the coast at Fanore. Sitting peaceably in the doorway, the collie politely moves quietly out of the way to allow customers to enter, obeying a sign above the door that warns: 'No dogs allowed on the premises. Management.'

One September morning I watched a dragonfly slowly dry

its wings in preparation for its daily aerial acrobatics. The swans seem to preen and indulge in wing-spreading at a tranquil pace. Herons lift on leisurely wings, slow-flapping their way into the air. The blackbird's song, especially in the evening, is relaxed with its soft lazy fluting pouring over the hills.

The Burren hares run but only after walking a few paces and even then seem to proceed in a series of slow springs not unlike a joey. For sheer daring nothing beats the wildlife encounter I once experienced on the road at Lisgoogan. For several minutes one day in June a leveret caused a traffic tailback on the road. The young hare, no more than six months old with long hind legs and light brown fur, surprised me on a straight stretch of road driving to Carron. I braked sharply, expecting it to run off at speed. But once it saw the car, instead of scampering, it started a gentle run, more of a slow-paced glide, down the middle of the road in a straight line not in any particular hurry to scurry off. I nudged the car forward a few metres, paused and watched it trying to work out its next move. My bemused passengers burst out laughing when it began a jig, twisting and turning, agonising over its route and changing its mind.

Like the pied piper it continued its easy-going run, decelerating, stopping again, casually looking around over its shoulder, eyes wide open, sizing up the metre-high stone walls on either side of the road, hesitating uncertainly for a few moments, gazing into a gap then thinking better of it before continuing its road journey. It was searching for an off-road opening and no gaps were visible in the tightly built walls, but the leveret gave the impression of not caring about finding one. Pausing again, turning right, then left, surveying the landscape, ears twitching, it carried on tarmac-bashing. Driving slowly behind it, keeping a 30m distance with a grandstand view, I again paused, stealing a glance in my rear view mirror. Behind me a cavalcade of a dozen cars, two minibuses and a coach load of tourists queued patiently. One man got out of his car, binoculars clamped to face. No one had any thoughts of overtaking and wanted to watch this spectacle in awe as though a high-definition TV nature programme was replaying before our eyes in real time.

Still not versed in the ways of the cruel world, the leveret clearly had no fear of humans or cars and had no qualms about its athletics interrupting the flow of traffic. It was trying carefully to select its exit point – all in its own time and at its own pace without pressure. After another thirty seconds of road running, more to-ing and fro-ing, it finally decided its merry dance was over. Jack-in-the-box like, it reared up on its hind legs springing through a small opening at the side of a gate, performing a slick disappearing trick.

All told, the Burren animal kingdom seems to pride itself on its love of *dolce far niente* – the sweet business of doing nothing, or, at least, giving the impression of doing very little. Other notes from my journals over the years, reflecting not just the animal world but the wider aspect, illustrate the point: a red and white rescue helicopter on its way to a mission at Fanore cliffs seems in no particular hurry. I watch its rotor blades move at a genteel pace. A navy trawler from Ballyvaughan harbour heading out into the wider waters of the Atlantic moves at a slow rate of knots causing only the smallest ripple in the water.

The sunsets have a delayed magnificence. On quiet days the sea is so calm it can look positively comatose. Waves slop lazily over boulders and rocks. The wind can be lazy too. It does not cut through you in the way that it grabs you in other parts of the west of Ireland. Stand on higher ground and it can surprise you but generally it does not provide the lift-you-off-your-feet experience that you get on a windy day at the top of O'Brien's Tower at the Cliffs of Moher.

There are few places where food is held in such awe and treated in such a dignified manner. In mid-May the Burren

Slow Food Festival in Lisdoonvarna attracts large crowds. Cookery demonstrations, farmers' markets and food talks as well as workshops for children's cooking are held, all in a relaxed manner. The summer torpor seems to affect visitors and locals alike. Tourists sip their hot flasks of tea and soup at an unhurried pace. A woman snoozes at the steering wheel lulled into a siesta at the beauty of it all. Two cyclists leisurely freewheel downhill, arms wide apart. And naturally enough the pint-pulling server will inform you that you cannot hurry the stout. For you must never forget: we are in the Burren. Time passes. Everything runs to its own dreamily slow geologic time. *Festina lente* – hurry slowly – whether cyclist, walker, driver or loveable leveret.

Facing page: Stonewall and bloody cranesbill © Marty Johnston

8

Grazing around Gleninagh

Touch the earth, love the earth, honour the earth, her plains,
her valleys, her hills, and her seas; rest in your spirit in her
solitary places. For the gifts of life are the earth's, and they are
given to all, and they are the songs of birds at daybreak, Orion
and the Bear, and dawn seen over ocean from the beach.

Henry Beston, *The Outermost House*

The strains of 'Amazing Grace' played *animato* on a
concertina float across the night air as a summer drizzle and
mist enfolds the townland of Gleninagh along the coast road
to Black Head. Fifty people of all ages pick their way carefully
through a grassy field for the annual pilgrimage to a holy well
said to cure eye infections. The Well of the Holy Cross, *Tobar
na Croise Naoimhe*, is tucked into a corner where the becapped
musical maestro Chris Droney from Bell Harbour is perched
atop a stone under a tree.

As the grey trestle tables are laid out for mass, the atmosphere
is hushed and reverent. Fr Des Forde welcomes the umbrellaed
and anoraked pilgrims standing hugger-mugger in a semi-circle

round the well. Several cars and a people carrier have been driven into the field. The sky has turned into a solid blanket of grey and the rain appears to be on for the evening. Although it looks uninviting, the murmur of the sea adds to the tranquil background.

The sixteenth-century well-house with its pointed-arch doorway shows signs of having been recently visited. Handkerchiefs and pieces of white rag cloth are tied to branches of the overhanging ash tree in which two pigeons are answering a higher call to prayer. The date is 3 August 2010 and for ten years Fr Forde has officiated at a revival of a centuries-old tradition of well-worship. I have gatecrashed the ecclesiastical outing to learn about its place in people's lives.

'The well is a symbol of our faith,' Fr Forde tells the pilgrims. 'We are 75 per cent water – perhaps a little bit more tonight – and this is a very special place that we've come to. Water is a powerful symbol and we are brought together in unity. There is power in being together and in walking down here and that is why the pilgrimage is important. This is a place of great energy. Just like getting petrol in your car you refuel, so in the same way you come to Gleninagh to be energised and refueled.'

He thanks the O'Donoghue and Scheunemann families who maintain the well. Unlike pilgrimages to many holy wells, Gleninagh does not hold a traditional ritual pattern called *deiseal* where people walk in clockwise circles repeating Hail Marys, Our Fathers or Glorias. The ceremony involves a structured mass with responses and Eucharistic sacrifice conducted like a church mass. After a biblical reading and a prayer, Chris picks up his concertina again and 'Lord of All Faithfulness' spurs an elderly woman to clutch her rosary beads. Two other women huddle together sharing an umbrella on the newly whitewashed stones surrounding the well. The drizzle continues unabated. A young couple beside me reflect on the weather.

'My socks are wringin'.'

'Put your mobile in your handbag, you can't answer it here,' comes the caustic reply.

Undeterred by the rain, the priest puts a positive spin on the dampness. 'The place where we live in is what matters. We need to make time for each other as we are always busy in this life. The rain will help us all to grow.'

He lapses into Irish then offers bread to worshippers. Wet hands are shaken in peace. Although I am standing on the margins he gives me a firm handshake and returns to his makeshift pulpit.

'Music,' he concludes, 'is a beatitude for us tonight and in the same way as Christ spoke to us, we are lifted by music and song.'

The resonance of his words hangs in the air for a few seconds, then on cue, and accompanied by a guitarist, Chris crackles into the first of three swift Clare jigs with great virtuosity: 'The Trip to the Cottage' followed by 'Scully's Fancy' and 'The Master's Return'. The volume is pumped up for the rousing 'Fiddler's Green' finale and by the end of the service the only dry thing left is Fr Forde's wit: 'You can all take your clothes off and get into the well if you like but you're invited firstly to come and partake of the hospitality wagon.'

Soul-cleansed, the pilgrims queue up at stalls laden with trays of salad, ham and cheese sandwiches. Strong tea is poured from large silver pots into china cups and biscuit tins passed around. Children drink lemonade and scoff cheese and onion crisps. Three young boys in football jerseys throw loose stones at each other beside the castle. Convivially we squelch around making the most of the mingle-opportunity, the music animating everyone. Fr Forde is a genial Galwegian with a sense of humour. After he came to Ballyvaughan and Fanore in 2001 he revived the pilgrimage. During our soggy supper he chats to me about how he sees pilgrimages fitting into life in the twenty-first century.

'By meeting and talking to each other people get a huge amount out of it,' he reflects. 'I walked down here from the pinnacle well along the main road and down a lane with a ninety-year-old woman who had no stick and no glasses. She is a retired teacher and we talked about things that are coming up in her life. It was a wonderful social and pastoral discussion with her.

'What has happened in general with pilgrimages is that it's not faith in a dogmatic kind of a way – it's not religious, but it's spiritual. There is no saint here but it was through the Cross that Christ rose and it's interesting that the Gleninagh blessed well is called the Well of the Holy Cross. A few years ago the cross was stolen so we did some fund-raising and have a new one that is now firmly embedded. Someone said to me tonight if it's going to be stolen again the thief will have to take the whole well. You'd be amazed at what people do – some of them would even take stones off your wall and plunder the limestone.'

We talk about the healing power of the well and the common practice of leaving rags tied to trees beside it. This is based on rubbing the diseased part of the body with the rag, then transferring the ailment to the rag which gradually leaves the body as the rag rots away. It has produced positive results for local people.

'A woman who had an eye problem used to visit the well and rub her eyes and it went away. That is not of course a scientifically proven miracle but nonetheless it cured her. There is a theory that I have heard people around here saying – that if you go to the well and you see an eel in it then that means that the healing potential is there. It is a lucky omen to see the eel although most people don't see it but this woman may have seen it. People keep going to the well in the hope of being healed and they have a very strong faith.'

Despite the persistent drizzle, the night air stimulates talk. People stand chatting in knots of three and four. Some shout greetings to each other, exchanging banter as though at a county agricultural show. Many who attend the ceremony grew up in the area and some still live here while others have moved away. John O'Donoghue, who was brought up in Gleninagh, moved to England in 1958 and now lives in Milton Keynes. He has returned specially for the pilgrimage and reminisces about life as a young boy.

'People didn't have very much back in the 1950s when I lived here,' he says. 'My father, who spoke Irish, was the last fisherman. There was a bit of fishing and farming and we played card games such as 25 and 45 but that was about it. Some people picked winkles and carrageen moss to make a few bob and then made jellies out of it. At one time there would have been more than a dozen currachs fishing off Gleninagh pier and their catch would have been sent to Limerick and Galway.'

John looks up at Gleninagh Castle and recalls the time in his childhood when a bullock once got inside and made its way up the stairway to the top. His father had to be called to help get it out.

Munching on his sandwiches, Pat Browne, who spoke at the end of the service, says he is impressed by the community spirit. He grew up in Gleninagh and now describes himself a 'permanent visitor'.

'Our family had a house here which was built by my grandfather who was Church of Ireland rector in Ennis. It was an impoverished area in the late 1940s and 1950s when I was a boy. There was no employment in those post-war days. Most young people left although there may have been one person in the family who was given the land and stayed on. What's interesting now is that quite a number have come back. It's changed now; in fact it's almost middle-class and quite refined whereas forty years ago it was a working and fishing area.'

Pat says it is called the Well of the Holy Cross because the whole area was under the ownership of the diocese of Kilfenora and therefore it came from the Bishop's Cross. His mother used to swim in the sea off Gleninagh every morning until she was in her eighties. Local tradition states that German submarines regularly refilled with water from the well.

'The well-water is very low down the table. It has a high mineral content and has a higher content of dissolved oxygen than most other places.'

By 9.30 p.m. many worshippers have left but a few linger as darkness closes in before making their way back up the lane to the road. Dampness permeates my clothes, shoes, notebook and thoughts. Across the bay the lights of Connemara are coming on, the sea is surly, the sky has turned dark and the summer stars are hidden. The ash tree which is ideally positioned somehow seems to belong perfectly to the history of the place. I step down to look into the well. A simple wooden cross says 'Seek Within'. Votive offerings, including small crosses, fragile waxed candles and jam-jars, have been placed by the faithful on shelf-rocks, and a cracked Mother and Child gaze out at me with untroubled serenity. In this treasured place of pilgrimage and prayer lie shells, white stones, coins and a red rose all in a small pool of dark water. Tonight, Gleninagh keeps the faith but the elusive eel is nowhere to be seen.

~~~

Two centuries ago more than 800 people lived and farmed in Gleninagh; today fewer than forty people live in this area. Over the years on visits to try to get to know it and read its history, I have taken time to potter and ponder and have come to realise the sense of loss and abandonment which is found here. There is sadness to strolling around the fields and in imagining how it once had been. Even the cows have a mournful bellow.

To get a feel for the atmosphere of Gleninagh, a wander around it will open your eyes to the human history and the flora to be found in one small patch of land. Gleninagh, *Gleann Eidhneach*, translates as 'Glen of the Ivy' and the last Irish speakers in County Clare lived here. The townland (one of 2,176 in Clare and spelled on some maps and in books as Glaninagh) is divided into two territorial divisions north and south, and is equidistant between Ballyvaughan and Black Head. There is no coastal hamlet or village, but it is made up of scattered cottages and houses along the roadside and down lanes. Gleninagh North sits hard by the sea on a rock-strewn shore. Incorporated within this area of a few square kilometres are a deserted village, an abandoned tower house, a derelict medieval parish church, and the remains of the site of Gleninagh Lodge along with other unidentified skeletal ruins including forts. Historical sites litter the ground. Apart from the holy well, a close inspection reveals an ancient cooking place and a lime kiln within a few metres of each other.

It can be approached by two ways: either walking down a gently sloping lane used by the pilgrims, or by boat from the sea, but tourist coaches do not stop here and few boats moor at the quay where the Earl of Ormonde sailed into exile in 1639. Parking nearby is difficult, so the area is neglected by visitors and remains one of the Burren's secrets. You will not find it in any modern guidebooks but in 1831 it was mentioned in Samuel Lewis' topography of Ireland. In the 1840s Thomas L. Cooke of Parsonstown, who wrote a series 'Autumnal Rambles about New Quay' for the *Galway Vindicator*, visited the well. He described its walls of solid masonry and the interior as 'having human skulls, and round flat stones resembling cakes of home-made bread'. It is also mentioned in *Murray's Handbook for Ireland*

(1906). The author John Cooke writes that at Gleninagh holy well a human skull was once used as a vessel for drinking but the practice was stopped by the parish priest.

Locals know its history and toponymy. Meet a farmer here and he will tell you that he comes from the townland of Gleninagh, in the parish of Ballyvaughan, in the diocese of Kilfenora, in the barony of the Burren, in the county of Clare, in the province of Munster, in the country of Ireland. Pride in place and in place names is etched deeply in the veins as firmly as the ferns rooted into Gleninagh's grykes.

There is much to see and admire. An axis of field-covered rocks and grass, a small wood, and the seashore thread through this ancient landscape. The ground is studded with a diverse flora. The range of flowers within a space the size of a football pitch includes scores of orchids, ferns and geraniums. On one spring visit I came across heath spotted-orchids and twayblade. Interwoven in this psychedelic mixed patch were the fluffy spikes of lady's bedstraw, Irish eyebright, wild thyme, kidney vetch, white clover and common milkwort, which, according to my guidebook, is known as 'the four sisters' because its flowers can be blue, pink, white or mauve. Buttercups, yellow-rattle, primroses, cowslips, yellow wort, and clusters of false oxlip all speckle the grass. Some plants are so inconspicuously coloured, many people never see them yet they have jewel-like quality. Look closely and you will identify speedwell, the slender St John's wort, and you may stumble upon the tiny but exquisite bee orchid whose blooms are startlingly lifelike imitations of bumble bees.

Hunkering along the woodland's edge, the grass is thick with sanicle, valerian, herb Robert and the vanilla-scented squinancy wort. The grykes house a striking selection of ferns: rusty-back, hart's-tongue and maidenhair spleenwort grow in sizeable clumps while wild madder and saxifrage colonise the clints and rocks. Along the seafront you will find bladder campion and thrift. These fields represent a bewildering array of resident species where every square inch of ground vibrates with a teeming mass of plant-life. It is the Burren showing off and few are aware of it.

Standing guard over all this botanical richness is the tall L-shaped tower of Gleninagh Castle, a waterside fort beside the well. It was built as a stronghold by the Ó Lochlainn family in the late sixteenth century. They disposed of it in the mid-1600s, but later regained ownership and were the last inhabitants when it was abandoned in 1840. The main block rises to five storeys, with stone-arched roofs over the first and third storeys. Rounded corner turrets are well preserved. The tower overlooks a stony beach and, with its high narrow windows, was an important coastal vantage-point from which to survey Galway Bay.

On one occasion, as part of a tour on a harsh winter's morning at seven o'clock, a key was produced and, ducking cobwebs, I made my way up a cramped mouldy spiral stairway. Liscannor slabs decorate the floor and the height lends a new perspective to gaze around Gleninagh through windowless frames and defensive slits. The early morning light could have been dirty concrete but out to sea, undeterred by the coldness, a great northern diver was enjoying itself in the steely grey water. Riding the waves unconcernedly with its head underwater, it bobbed up to allow me to catch a glimpse through binoculars of its thick neck, dagger-like beak and sleek body. My grandstand view was obscured by morning mist. But farther round the coast I could just make out the fat punctuation mark of the Martello tower at the tip of the Flaggy Shore. The castle is one of the Burren's most evocative look-out points and it is not hard to understand why the builders chose this site lording over the stones, sea and bay.

The Burren boasts numerous ruins among its notable

architectural glories but few can compare with the well-appointed condition of Gleninagh Castle, which is still in a surprisingly sound state given its 400-year-old pedigree. Birds have haunted this building and the seashore for centuries. The sense of abandonment is again apparent as in the 1990s it was home to red-beaked choughs. They have since vanished and been replaced by the clatter of rock doves (west of Ireland progenitors of wild pigeons) now frequenting the dank corners.

Through a field thick with thistles and clover, I make my way over to the cracked limestone shoreline passing the remains of an outdoor cooking area (*fulacht fiadh*). There is evidence of the remains of a lime kiln where the whitewash was prepared to paint the tower house. Thousands of smooth stones along the shorefront have taken themselves down for a swim where the sea comes in unwhitened by foam. In the bright Gleninagh light, they glisten with a distinctly luminous quality.

Back up towards the main road, the ancient Gleninagh churchyard lies roofless and largely unnoticed behind a stone wall. Long strands of ivy cling to one wall while brightly purpled buddleia rises up along another. Spiders' webs are woven around wall rue growing profusely over the stones. T. J. Westropp visited it during his travels around Clare describing it as 'a rude plain building with a pointed south door, lintelled south window and round-headed east window'.

It presents a sad unkempt appearance today although a watering can and waste bin augur well for a tidy up. Moss covers knee-high nameless stumps of headstones or ones where inscriptions have been worn away with the years. I had been told that bodies of washed up sailors were buried here alongside graves that may include famine victims but none are marked. The twentieth-century gravestone names include Donohue, McCarthy, Burns, Irwin, Fitzpatrick, O'Donoghue, and come from Gleninagh, Ballyconry and Ballyvaughan.

A short walk across the road is the deserted village of Creig, not far from the pinnacle well. The crumbling stone remains are overgrown with a mini-forest of nettles, weeds and vegetation along with a tangle of twenty worn tractor and car tyres. I trample them down and walk over to inspect the cavities where the fireplaces once stood. Other signs reflect the surviving evidence of human habitation that is all part of the awe-inspiring character of this place.

Look up towards the terraced Gleninagh Mountain brooding over the area and you will make out the faint trace of a mass path running through a gap in the hills leading up to the southern limit of the area of our exploration: Gleninagh South. From the wayside cairn near the roadside, I take a stony path diverting to the top of Gleninagh Mountain (*Cnoc Achadh na Glinne*) which, as Irish mountains go, is not high. At 318m in stature, it qualifies as the Burren's joint highest point along with the neighbouring hill of *Dobhach Bhrainin* a short limestone hop away. Sit quietly for a while on the summit beside the Ordnance Survey triangulation pillar; soon you will appreciate the absence of noise and will be afforded a wide panorama of sea and landscape embracing Galway Bay, the islands, and the far shore of Connemara.

The mass path runs for over 3km, leading steadily uphill and downhill, eventually merging with the Burren Way, a signposted route favoured by hillwalkers. All around, and on the periphery of Gleninagh South, the past snatches at you: another deserted village here, a penal chapel there, and at Caheranardurrish the ruins of a mass house and shebeen at the point of entry into the haunting Caher Valley.

There is another human tragedy here; a heart-breaking story of how, in the middle part of the twentieth century, many people fled this area after an outbreak of tuberculosis swept through it. TB was rampant in many parts of Ireland and Gleninagh suffered acutely, resulting in mass emigration from this once populous area.

Since I first stumbled on Gleninagh on a coastal walk, it is a place I have constantly been pulled back to, poking around an area preserved in a mix of aspic and cow dung. It has a quiet reserve with a piquancy and element of mystery. It conceals itself, hiding its sad history, shy about flaunting its enigmatic past (apart from a signboard at the castle, no written information about the area is on display). The stranger must dig deep to explore and uncover the bristling layers.

Apart from an occasional farmer checking on his livestock and the annual well-worshippers, I rarely meet other people here. Few who come to the Burren have seen or smelt it, soaked themselves in its past or tested its present-day religious and musical pulse. The absence of visitors gives it the idyllic feel of west of Ireland solitude. This is a place where the light stretches long on clear summer evenings, lingering over the hills, fields and sea, where the moonlight mingles with the pink sunset. Stand on Gleninagh's stones facing the sea, look across the bay to Connemara and you may experience a dream-like quality to the light. As you do, think of the intricate interplay of the dead and the living cultures imbued within this townland. I like to reflect on the generations that have preceded me and the ghostly echoes of the past surrounding me.

On each visit I have gleaned new fragments containing individual snippets of information to try to build a partial jigsaw of the concatenation of historical events and the shifting rhythms of life of this sliver of land. It is remarkable how one small pocket covering some rough fields can pulsate with so many eras. If you wish to feel the quivers of the multiple layers, long vistas and powerful continuity of history, as well as sampling the array of exotic flora, all you need do is spend some time at Gleninagh where the past is continuously at your elbow. Look around these memory-filled fields and you will feel the power of an older world linked to the present in a unique history-sodden combination of people, plants and piety in an atmosphere drenched in melancholy, and occasionally, music.

Gleninagh holy well © Trevor Ferris

9

Travels of the Wandering Rocks

Patient observation and constant brooding above the rocks,
lying upon them for years as the ice did, is the way to arrive at
the truths which are graven so lavishly upon them.

John Muir, 'John of the Mountains'

'What in tarnation,' the man from Kentucky asks, 'is an erratic?' He had been listening to a brief description of how these huge grey boulders came to be placed on the limestone pavement. His fellow Americans are in awe of the history all around them.

No one has ever counted how many of these boulders, known as glacial erratics, are scattered throughout the Burren. It would be a colossal task because thousands of them were carried here by glaciers and deposited as if by magic. Today these peculiar features of the landscape – both limestone and granite – sit peaceably at rest from their travels, rock solid, or in some places, perched precariously on disproportionately small pedestals of bedrock that have been protected from erosion. From a distance some look as though they could be toppled with a nonchalant shove, or easily rolled down a hillside and pushed into the sea. In truth it would take an army of strong Burren men and women to shift these enormous boulders whose weights vary but tip the scales at an average of ten tons. Too tough to break up into small stones, they have been left standing and are now integrated as part of the outdoor décor. They have stood here for 15,000 years and despite some weathering have retained their shape. Now they stand alone, immovable, monolithic, and at first sight, unremarkable and commonplace. But despite their mute appearance, they are a special topographical feature and come with a story all their own.

The word erratic is from the Latin *errare* meaning 'to wander'. Over the course of my visits I have often spent time on a wandering, rock-hopping quest to see how many I could locate. First there was bird-spotting, then train-spotting . . . but erratic-spotting? From the roadside, erratics can be hard to pick out, camouflaged into the limestone and blending into the interminable succession of grey drystone walls and bare pavement. But when you get close it is a different story. A walk across the large flat slabs of pavement uncovers scores of these historic natural rock monuments. One of the best areas for this search is Black Head. Many of the Carboniferous limestone erratics abandoned here were picked up by glaciers from across Galway Bay. As the ice-floe advanced southwards across the bay, it ripped up great lumps of rock, rolled them round in the glacier and, when it melted, dumped them unceremoniously on the Burren. Other erratics come from Galway granite on the far side of the bay while the old Dalradian rocks of Connemara were also transported southwards.

In a morning's walk at Black Head I count more than seventy-five. They are spread in a seemingly haphazard, incongruous jumble, but in places there is an order to their curvilinear symmetry. Beside a low stone wall threading its way down from

Murroughkilly, a line of erratics known as a boulder-streak is visible. They are often found aligned as the glaciers moved in a long train stringing them out in a continuous curving line. A large, potato-shaped erratic provides the ideal rock-steady resting place for a lunch break and the chance to appreciate the juxtaposition of hills and sea. It also affords one of the best places for a sense of the infinite. Beside a wall, a hare stands alert, listens to the wind, gives an abrupt turn of the head and jinks off, zigzagging its way across the pavement.

I have come to know the Black Head erratics – not so much on first-name terms – but more as reference points from which I depart and return with confidence on each visit. Having acquired their strange forms and locations in my mind I have brought photographers and groups here, pointing out the boulder-streak, explaining how it helped me to work out how the erratics came to be here, informing my pathway of understanding. Silhouetted against the darkening sky, they look unnerving to some but for me they define the spirit of this place and in particular a specific spot at Murrough where the dark green needle-shaped leaves of a sprawling juniper bush sprout, often with small yellow cones, from a gryke.

Erratics are chemical rocks that contain fossils called colonial coral. They have lots of corals growing together. Some have veins, others have dolomite and chert, which is similar to flint and is a silica. It was much sought after by early settlers in Ireland. In the early nineteenth century, geologists were mystified by the boulders they found throughout Europe and which were different in composition from their surroundings. It was thought they were carried to their destinations by currents of water and mud associated with Noah's flood.

So much for their provenance – what do these stone giants look like today? Geologists describe erratics as a 'flat-iron' shape. They have a humped back and a flat bottom with a pointed end and a steep end which is how they got the name. Apart from the flat-iron description, many have a characteristic potato shape, but they are not uniform in appearance and vary greatly in size. In some places they have a striking individuality and an anthropomorphic sense about them. Intriguingly, as I discover on an exploration of their sculptural expressions, it is as if they have been chiselled in a certain way and each has an identity peculiar to itself. Some have comical lichened faces, a few wear frowns; some look sad or baleful, others have a smiling countenance, happy with their geological lot perched on their pedestal of contentment. One or two of these leviathans resemble the shape of a shark or whale; another, standing next door to a more traditionally erect one, looks for all the world like a giant slumbering tortoise. Two others could be mistaken for a camel and a monkey. This phenomenon – known as pareidolia – is a delusion based on sense perception of seeing a human face or another form in an inanimate object. Some look unbalanced, out of kilter with a warped appearance and an anguished face. Another has a carved face similar-looking to the flat and steep forehead physiognomy of an Easter Island statue staring out to sea. With its nose, mouth, bold jaw and Negroid head, it stands in silent testimony – a stony-faced sentry – looking out to the Aran Islands moored far out in the Atlantic. Buffeted by storms, rain and sea showers, the lashing gales are of no consequence to these boulders. They have seen them off, weathered the storm and stuck fast to their base. Like polished diamonds, some gleam in the sunlight with a smooth curvature, others have an ungainly shape sculpted by the elements.

Black Head is not the only area where erratics are found. They are everywhere: on the northern slopes of Slieve Elva, halfway up other hills, on many sections of the flat limestone, along the sea front, on the shingle and sand, and 32km inland at Mullaghmore. My hunt takes me south along the coast to

Poll Salach where the erratics plunge towards the sea. Here they have a scruffier look. Their texture is a darker, blacker volcanic consistency, pockmarked and aerated with bubbles, riddled with the geological equivalent of woodworm, and crumbling with cracks. They lack the roundedness of their more northerly or inland brethren. Running my fingers over the surface, I find they are heavily colonised by moss and encrusted with close-growing lichen, ranging in shade from a palette of tangerine through to orange, yellow and silver blotches. Cushions of pink sea thrift and the pale creams of sea campion surround their base. At the far end of the limestone at Poll Salach, one resembles a chipmunk with a funny nose.

Not surprisingly after 15,000 years in one spot, some are showing their age. Since being placed here they have shrunk a little and over the centuries a small amount of weathering has affected them. Once exposed to the elements, they start to dissolve with rainwater and develop cracks through both the cold and the heat. Erratics suffer biological erosion, mechanical erosion, and chemical erosion and in some cases the algae and ragged tufts of lichen living on them are grinding parts of them very slowly into powder underneath. The lichens I have come across include map lichen, richly patterned yellow scales lichen and sea ivory, a tufted and branched lichen on rocks and walls which is tolerant of salt spray.

In the central southern portion of the Burren a forlorn erratic at Sheshymore presides proudly on a clint, aloof and alone, the epitome of firmness in the middle of a large, flat, crisscross oasis of pavement. Its solitariness accentuates the loneliness of the place. Its base is decorated with clusters of milkwort and magenta geraniums. Early purple orchids up to 20cm tall blow in regal richness in the gentle wind, and holly and ivy are entwined within its crevices.

'See one rock, see them all,' said Socrates; not so erratics

– they are uniquely different. In the extreme southeast, beside Mullaghmore Mountain, boulders on a grand scale line the pavement in fellowship, offering a variety of styles and shapes for the anorak erratic spotter or those smitten by the rock. Along the road between Treanmanach and Cooloorta, in the aptly named Rock Forest, they sit placidly beside and, in several instances, embedded in stone walls helping to hold them together. Some lean at curious angles of repose on the pavement and around the edges of a turlough with the distinctive whorls of the ordered staircase terracing a dramatic backdrop. Others are smooth and fissured with black, cream and honey-yellow blotches or garlanded with moss and lichen. A small number have a slimmer, leaner look, with indents and long, slender holes the length of a pencil. A few are diamond-shaped with bits chipped off. Another, a figure of eight, is surrounded by the bright bird's-foot trefoil at its base while a neighbouring one is grinning widely with what seems to be a curled lip. The Rock Forest floor is a graveyard of randomly situated erratics. I have often wondered about the collective noun for them. Perhaps a 'havoc' of boulders would best characterise them at Mullaghmore, although a 'settlement' or even an 'abandonment' of erratics somehow seems more permanently appropriate.

Not far away, lying to either side of Lough Gealáin, at Rinnamona and Gortlecka, you will find a variation on the erratic theme – possibly cousins or second cousins (non-geological family terms) but clearly a different category. These easily overlooked curiosities are known as mushroom or wave stones and are water-worn limestone blocks standing up to 3m high. As their name suggests their shape was caused by wave action over thousands of years.

In the Burren's eastern corner, at Keelhilla, Eagle's Rock towers over a trio of precariously balanced, gravity defying erratics. One rests on two stones on a pedestal, another sits on a plinth the shape of a pot plant holder and the third member of the party reclines at an angle with wedges. Some have veins, fissures and patches of grass with pebbles on top. At the easternmost range of the limestone a solitary erratic sits on the edge facing inland, guarding the entrance to the Burren on the approach from the New Line keeping a wary eye out for strangers.

The final contemplative leg of my tour of these rock refugees from another era ends appropriately at a long and skinny finger of land known as the Rine that reaches into the sea on the outskirts of Ballyvaughan. Looking out across Galway Bay and watching the play of light, I try to visualise the ice sheets that moved over this stretch of sea in a straight line, taking everything in its wake. It was a mighty cornucopia of noise and colour blazing its way relentlessly across and, like an angry giant, depositing missiles many kilometres away from their point of origin. The glacier has been gone a long time but its handiwork is still apparent. A pair of cormorants speeds across the top of the bay interrupting my thoughts. Farther out to sea a boat slowly trails white-foam wakes across the turquoise ocean. Water laps round the base of a suite of small erratics. They share a stony beach and fields along this spit of land with fat cattle and a silent, thin-legged horse and foal. Standing among shells and seaweed, as well as a tangle of nettles, ox-eye daisies, primroses, herb Robert, thistles and dandelions, they appear much more angled and flatter. Some of the Rine erratics have an off-white delicate coating; these particular bundles – neat, creamy circles of limeaceous splay – are the signature of countless seabirds swooping in over the coastline.

Choose any part of this stark landscape that takes your fancy, go with the flow and you will find your own favourite boulder posing on its final resting place in splendid isolation. Some are of such importance that on the map you will even find them individually marked. Whatever their names and appearance, whatever their imagined expressions, they all have – unlike the American visitors – one historic fact in common: these totems have given up the vagaries of a wandering life in favour of a sedentary existence and look as though they will be in situ for thousands of years to come.

Boulder-streak at Murrough, Black Head © Marty Johnston

10

A Woman for all Seasons

We simply need that wild country available to us, even if we
never do more than drive to its edge and look in. For it can be
a means of reassuring ourselves of our sanity as creatures, a part
of the geography of hope.

Wallace Stegner, *Wilderness Letter*

For more than twenty-three years Ireland's sole contribution
to a small column tucked away at the bottom of an inside
page of one of Britain's national daily newspapers came from
the Burren. No more than 350 words long and taking just five
minutes to read, the Country Diary in the *Guardian* featuring
wildlife notes from different regions of Ireland and Britain, has
a loyal following. The contributors write with flair about the
fluctuations of the countryside, the weather, the migration of
birds, or a particular aspect of the outdoors that interests them. It
could be the depth of the winter snow in the Scottish Highlands,
the cloud formations over Cadair Idris in mid-Wales, the whistle
of an otter in Peeblesshire, or the antics of badgers in the Lake
District.

Between 1987 and 2010 Sarah Poyntz wrote monthly dispatches with knowledge and passion about the Burren. Taking the reader on a journey, she walked the green roads and the seashore, studied the wildlife, checked on the flora, observed the changing seasons, and had a friendly gossip about the weather with her neighbours. All these encounters were squeezed into a condensed and easily readable slot.

When you have had your fill of revolutions, coups, famine, economic depression, the turmoil of government and political squabbling, you can turn to the Country Diary, memorably described by its editor as 'a touchstone of sanity'. It is indeed an oasis in a troubled world, a restful way to start your day. Transport yourself to a specific area, close your eyes and quietly imagine the scene being created by these wildlife wordsmiths. Originally called the Country Lover's Diary, the column has been running continuously since 1904. The contributors have included illustrious names such as William Condry who wrote the *New Naturalist Guide to Wales*, and A. Harry Griffin, a regular diarist for a staggering fifty-three years and author of many books on the Lakeland hills.

In all weathers, in all seasons Sarah evocatively documented the moods of the Burren in its infinite richness, entertaining readers from the Orkneys to Oxford and from Penzance to Portarlington. An instinctive observer, her skill was in capturing the character of individual species and describing what makes the place special for her and her friends.

To see the place through the eyes of someone who has lived here for a long time, I joined her for a walk across the limestone not far from her home overlooking Ballyvaughan Bay. Her delight in the place that she adopted as home is obvious. For many years she had been an admirer of the *Guardian* column and expressed an interest in becoming a diarist. The editor asked her to send an example of her writing but warned her not to hold out much hope as more than 300 people were on a waiting list to write a column.

'I simply sent off a sample diary,' she says, 'and got a phone call to say they had selected me because they wanted someone from Ireland. So in January 1987 I began writing the column and wrote my final one in December 2010.'

We walk along the shorefront near her cottage climbing over a low drystone wall passing primroses, cowslips and violets. Sarah pauses on an unsteady clint identifying within a few metres of each other the dazzling purple petals of bloody cranesbill, the fluorescent yellow vividness of bird's-foot trefoil, kidney vetch, hoary rockrose, and large clumps of spring sandwort flourishing in a spectrum of colours. Field glasses in hand, she points up to the rounded top of Cappanawalla behind her cottage and its stepped terracing where the cattle spend the winter.

'I love the Burren because the air is so pure. It has wound itself round my heartstrings since I retired here in the mid-1980s.'

Originally from New Ross in County Wexford, Sarah taught English in Cornwall and Cambridge, later spending time writing and travelling in the US. It took her several years to believe her good fortune that she had found the perfect place to live on the Clare coast. Since then, she has never ceased to be amazed at the wonder of the Burren. Many of her best ideas are found simply by walking and exploring the fields and roads or the ruins of an abbey or church.

'Sometimes you don't even need to leave the house. It's inspirational just looking out through our window on to the sea and across to Finavarra and the Flaggy Shore. I read a lot about the Burren and about the fascinating wildlife that we have and it all just seemed to come together. It's such a beautiful place. When I was writing the diary I never made notes when I was out walking but instead wrote it in my head. I would go back home, start working on it, jotting down what I'd seen, putting the date on it, letting it simmer in my mind, and then writing about it.'

Sarah has always enjoyed the research involved, constantly checking facts or dates, finding out about some of the lesser-known flowers, or the quirky habits of the stoat, pygmy shrew or feral goats. 'I'm not a professional biologist or botanist but I have bought a lot of books and I supplemented the articles with information from these.'

Characteristically thorough in her research she always wrote her diary in pencil in a pad and typed it on to a computer, sometimes cutting it back or embellishing it. She then checked and rechecked, omitting needless words, before sending off her polished précis to London where they appeared on the leader page, the paper's most respected section.

'There was a great brouhaha when the paper changed the format to the Berliner style and we were told to write 400 words but it got settled back down again to 350. Every word and letter had to count – even the letter "a". But it was satisfying producing a good diary in a concise style and one of the nice things about writing was getting letters from *Guardian* readers.

Not only did I get fan mail but I also got what I call fan persons coming to the door. They enquire in the shops where I live, then I get a phone call and people ask if they can come and see me. Sometimes they buy my book and ask me to sign it. They were from various parts of Britain and Ireland and when the diary appeared in the international paper, *The Guardian Weekly*, I used to get Americans coming. They were very kind and said they loved my diaries. Normally, as a writer, you don't get any feedback so it was great to get human feedback. When the readers admired the Burren itself through the words I've written it's nice that I've been able to pass it on and that they have taken the trouble to come and see it themselves.'

Each year Sarah wrote thirteen columns recording the

comings and goings of nature. 'It's hard to get the *Guardian* in Ballyvaughan. On one occasion when I picked it up, the diary had been cut so much I did not recognise it and there was no sense to it. I had a good rapport with the editors although once when I wrote about the caves I got the impression from the editor that they wanted it to be dumbed down, or at least to be made easy. The editor said it was rather academic, but it wasn't a bit academic, and that was annoying. The extraordinary thing was I had five letters from people saying they loved that particular piece.'

A strong literary flavour peppered many of her diaries. She loved to quote writers and poets and is extremely well versed. Frequently she invoked the words of Yeats, Chaucer, Keats or Ralph Waldo Emerson. 'I feel they really give us nature in such a marvellous unified way in terms of capturing the beauty of the world. They certainly hit the nail on the head. I love the naturalness of Yeats' poetry and the concept he gives of life without any stilt about it. It flows so beautifully. He was a tremendous thinker and I feel he hasn't got much credit for that. I also like the natural history work of Seamus Heaney and Michael Longley who've both written poems about the Burren.'

The author Eudora Welty, who wrote short stories, novels and essays about the American South, has also been an influence. Welty had a love of nature and an understanding of human nature, and she has a place in Sarah's pantheon of favourite writers. 'I came to know her work when I was in the States during the 1980s. Welty said she lived "a sheltered life" and except for short periods, she lived it in the house her parents built in Jackson, Mississippi. Her masterpiece is held to be *The Optimist's Daughter*, which won the Pulitzer Prize in 1973. I appreciate her writing because it is understated and her style is pure and very fine. She writes of places she knows such as her hometown Jackson, and does so with a humane elegance and delightful humour.'

Welty's object in writing, says Sarah, quoting directly from her, was to 'enter into the mind, heart, and skin of a human being who is not myself. Whether this happens to be a man or a woman, old or young, with skin black or white, the primary challenge lies in making the jump itself. It is the act of a writer's imagination that I rate most high.'

A quintessential diary by Sarah begins with an engaging quotation or reflects a moment of weather or wildlife drama. Some examples of opening lines include: 'That it should come to this', 'Yesterday and last night we had a mighty Atlantic storm', 'Poor Nellie is dead', 'Our house was wrapped in fog', 'At last! I never thought the time would come'.

Looking back on the hundreds of diaries she has written over the years Sarah says the one she is most proud of was in February 1999 which starts: 'Two surprises and two alarms as I walked under Cappanawalla Mountain', and includes two quotes, one from Shakespeare and one from Keats.

'It was about my meeting with a herd of wild goats below Cappanawalla Mountain. It encapsulated almost everything that I love about the Burren – animals, landscape, plants but lacked birds.'

With a glint in her eye Sarah admits to some special places that she has kept to herself. 'I have one or two little secrets and there is one place that is so beautiful. It's a small area of about 20cm square and it's in a wall. I think I'm the only person who has found it and knows about it and I keep it to myself. I look at it through every season. Small ferns and flowers grow in it . . . but I can't disclose its location because then it wouldn't be a secret.'

Sarah did not specialise in any particular topic but tackled a variety of subjects, throwing into her Burren recipe on occasions a dash of geology, archaeology, history, and local folklore.

'Sometimes I got a clue from other papers and used something that I've read about elsewhere and later checked myself. I also included birds because they are such an important element of life here. The sea too has played a big part in my writing. I just have to look out and no matter what the weather is like I get inspiration from the colours, the physical aspect of it, or in the depths of winter when it's roaring with a tempest.'

In all the years that she has been living in the Burren Sarah has seen many changes – not, in her view, for the better. 'Ballyvaughan is a special place but it has developed very badly over the years and sometimes I despair but I try not to convey that despair to my readers because I think there is enough doom and gloom around. I prefer the positive, happy and beautiful things rather than the opposite. They built nice little town houses in the centre of the village but there is another building near us that I think is absolutely disgraceful. It should never have even got planning permission. In the preparation of the site huge ten-metre-long clints of pavement were lifted up by an earth shifter, put into a machine and ground down into fist-sized stones. It nearly broke my heart to see that. In the end I had to drive past it without looking it was so dreadful. I think the county council and indeed the government is disgraceful at times.

'In Bell Harbour they've built holiday homes that are like rabbit hutches and are terrible. Domestic architecture in the Republic of Ireland is disgraceful. They have built houses three and four storeys high in the middle of rural Ireland and there is no excuse for it. It was just sheer ostentation. Some people had too much money and didn't know what to do with it so they showed off.'

Despite her dislike for these developments, the Burren still holds a magical appeal. Its seasons have provided her with a tremendous variety of descriptive copy but she finds it hard to single one out.

'I don't have a favourite season. Then sometimes I rethink

this and when the spring arrives this is my favourite. But when it's over, the summer comes and I call it the blue and purple season and I love it too. With the arrival of autumn we get the spareness of it all and it is beautiful. Winter shows the Burren in its bare rock with the bare branches of the trees and I especially love the sea in all its wildness.

'The quality of the light is special. That is one of the things that made it easy to write about because the landscape is changing all the time. I have a friend from Cornwall who came to paint here but the landscape changed so rapidly that she couldn't paint it because of the shadows and light passing so quickly. Although she did some pencil sketches, she couldn't capture it in a painting on canvas as it was too hard to do that. Some painters who come here adopt a more abstract, surreal feel for it. When it rains here it disappears quickly because of the porous landscape whereas in other areas this isn't the case. The biggest appeal is the beauty of the place and the naturalness of its people whose families have lived here for generations.'

Curiously, for someone living in the midst of a vast array of unique Arctic-alpine plants, when pushed to select her favourite, Sarah is a galanthophile and therefore chooses a modest flower – the humble common snowdrop or as Alfred, Lord Tennyson referred to it: 'the solitary firstling'.

'I love them all, of course,' she says, with a cheery sweep of her arms. 'The gentians, mountain avens, and the early purple orchids but when I see a single snowdrop early in the year rising from the stony ground then I realise the rest are on the way. There aren't that many snowdrops here but for me they are full of hope for what lies ahead.'

Sarah's writing has been published in *A Burren Journal* (2000), which is illustrated with delicate watercolours by Gordon D'Arcy and Anne Korff. In 2005 she wrote *Memory Emancipated*, a memoir of growing up in New Ross in the

1930s and early 1940s. She has also compiled and edited *Burren Villages: Tales of History and Imagination*, an anthology of essays about different aspects of the Burren published in 2010.

Although Sarah's swansong diary was penned on 9 December 2010, she has no intention of giving up observing, thinking and writing about the landscape on her doorstep. 'The Country Diaries opened up all the Burren for me from Mullaghmore to the coast and right across to the Gort lowlands. When I began writing them I was delighted with the welcome and encouragement I received from my first editors Chris McLean and Jeannette Page. They gave me freedom to write in the way I wanted to. Of course there is a certain sadness about ending something that gives great pleasure, but ends, as well as beginnings, have to be faced. And after all, I still have my beloved Burren and its splendid people.'

Like Wordsworth's daffodils, Sarah is 'jocund company', and a sprightly walk with her across the limestone reawakens a sense of wonder and exhilaration. For twenty-three years, as the only Irish correspondent, she occupied a unique place in the rich tradition of the eccentricities of country diarists. Her stealthy observations and finely honed affectionate vignettes of Burren life that decorated the columns of the *Guardian* opened up the area for many people who would otherwise not have known of it. An engrossing chronicle of the area, they collectively represent a unique snapshot of local history and lore. Written in a personable style, Sarah's diaries spoke – and still speak enduringly through her anthology – to somebody, somewhere in the world, and her personality shines through. Her peeps into local life, the vagaries of the weather, idiosyncratic snippets of local gossip, and the natural curiosities coupled with her evocative word painting gave pleasure to a wide and avid readership.

For her final diary she went for a walk through the Corker Pass between Abbey Hill and Turlough Hill witnessing 'the most

perfect rainbow' interrupted by a flash of lightning. In response
she spoke aloud to herself, 'This, our Burren, is beautiful beyond
compare.'

Sarah Poyntz, retired Burren *Guardian* country
diarist at her home at Ballyconry © Trevor Ferris

11

The Music of the Sea

Hug the shore, let others keep to the deep.

Virgil, *Aeneid*

New Quay Aperitif

Day One: Thursday evening 27 May 2006

Six pints of stout are slowly settling on the bar counter beside
two collection boxes, one for the South African Missions, the
other on behalf of Clarecare for the elderly and families in
need, 'Making Clare a better place'. A sign on the wall reads:
'Please – No Smoking, No Dancing, No Swearing. This is a
Respectable House.' The shelves hold a cream mug with five
Hamlet cigars and miniature bottles of Campari and Powers.
You can buy toothpicks, cigarette lighters and watercolour
postcards of the bar. In the next room Crunchie, Mars and Kit
Kat bars are available to wash down with your stout. The de
rigueur bar-room wall accessories include a large framed sketch
of the Poulnabrone dolmen stone, a touring map of the area,

and a Seamus Heaney poem, mounted and framed, celebrating the Flaggy Shore.

Looking like an after-thought to the northern part of the Burren, the Flaggy Shore on the Finavarra peninsula is a thin prong of land leading to a tower commanding the entrance to Ballyvaughan Bay. It also leads to one of Clare's finest pubs, Linnane's at New Quay. Consider the facts: you can enjoy your prawn open sandwich sitting outside on the back porch and, as you watch the oystercatchers at the pier, a low dappling sun settles over Galway Bay. Alternatively you can sit inside by the turf fire cradling a pint in a convivial atmosphere. I have come here to start the first leg of a walk along the whole of the Burren coastline down to Doolin, hugging the shore, keeping an eye out for birds and flowers, keeping the sea on my right hand side throughout the walk, and keeping music at the forefront of my mind.

The Irish traditional tunes are served up in a corner of Linnane's by an easy-going father-and-daughter combination on concertinas. A heady cocktail of reels, jigs, waltzes and hornpipes is pouring from the doughty duo. With exceptionally deft cross-key fingering, the tunes vary from reels to slow airs that strum the heart strings. The father opens each number with a solo introduction and after a few bars nods a smiling glance to his daughter who, with effortless ease and grace, intuitively picks up the melody. They stretch and squeeze their instruments unobtrusively, largely unnoticed, and unappreciated. Opposite them, a tall angular fiddler on a three-legged stool lies sleeping, slumped across the table. His hand supports his head. He nods forward occasionally, pulling himself back with a myoclonic jerk. An unfinished half-pint of stout languishes in his glass. Stickers on his black case on the floor say 'Up Clare' and 'Custy's Music Shop, Ennis'. Small groups of T-shirted, potbellied and ruddy-faced farmers with rascally charm stand around the bar in an easy camaraderie. Some laugh at him and prod his back;

he doesn't move a muscle. By one o'clock the turf fire has died, the music has died and the non-fiddler of New Quay looks as if he has died too. Draped around the shoulders of two men he is limply carted off and tossed into the back of a transit van, missing a glorious full moon that has risen, large and round, over the Flaggy Shore.

Day Two: Friday 28 May

I have based myself at Mount Vernon, a Georgian seaside villa and the summer home of Augusta Lady Gregory, a pivotal figure in the Irish cultural renaissance. This historic house was built in an unusual vernacular style and the owners, Mark Helmore and Ally Raftery, boast they do not have worldly interferences such as telephones, television or tea-making facilities in the bedrooms. Original features of the house from Lady Gregory's time include three fireplaces designed and built by the painter Augustus John who, along with W. B. Yeats and George Bernard Shaw, was a regular visitor. The cypress trees in the garden are said to have been the gift of George Washington.

From my bow-fronted bedroom window, I peer out through vermilion frames to a depressing grey day and a sea with small wavelets drained of its colours. The forecast promises wind and rain. A yellow-anoraked couple walks down the coast road with a brown and white collie running furiously ahead of them, pink tongue lolling from the side of his mouth. The dog pauses to survey the wind-capped waters of Aughinish Bay and watch swallows bustling about energetically. A mist restricts visibility out to sea.

Fanned by the Atlantic wind, I set off early on a rising spring tide along the northern coast of the Flaggy Shore. Swathed in mist, the lower tiers of terracing on the Burren hills look cold and uninviting. Masses of knee-high, bright yellow sea radish

lines the roadside as I drop down over a wall and across stones
to the seashore. A cormorant passes low across the surface of the
water with an early-morning sense of urgency as though late for
an important date. The recent heavy rain and the seaweed add
to the slipperiness of the rocks. I join a ready-made limestone
pavement path with shallow pools of water running parallel with
the rocks. A car passes with headlights on, and the breeze-ruffled
Lough Murri is birdless, duckless and swanless. A tan coastal
varnish, with clinging bladder wrack, covers the wave-scoured
rocks and boulders.

Once I cross a short portion of sandy and stony beach, the
distinctive shape of the Martello tower at Finavarra Point comes
into view. A hare bounds over a stone wall, leapfrogs across
my path, and disappears at breakneck speed into a ploughed
field. The tower is a well-preserved solid circular structure built
during the Napoleonic Wars of 1812–1816. A sign says: 'The
property including the Martello Tower and Appurtenances was
bequeathed to the state for the benefit of the Nation by Mrs
Maureen Emerson who died on the 4th day of November 1999.'

The sign does not mention the benefit to the rooks enjoying
its higher reaches. A robin comes to rest beside me on the
stones. I consult the map and realise that in just over an hour
I have covered the merest fraction – an infinitesimal amount –
and head swiftly for Scanlan's Island along the Flaggy Shore's
southern side. I disturb a family of whimbrels that rises quickly.
Just before I reach the breakwater, I come across a brightly
painted house standing on its own overlooking a lagoon. I had
read about an English artist who had painted strips of colour
along the walls of Pond House. A blue and white yacht *Lauren*
is tied up and the *Cherokee* speedboat sits on concrete blocks
raised off the ground. The peace is broken by the darting and
harsh twittering of a flock of sand martins that has established
a colony here.

The Cistercian Abbey at Corcomroe completed
in the early 13th century © Marty Johnston

Darkness descending over the Rock Forest,
Mullaghmore © Trevor Ferris

Above: Herb Robert on the limestone pavement © Marty Johnston

Right: Signpost at the T-junction, Ballyvaughan © Marty Johnston

A shower blows quickly in and over the lagoon. To avoid a detour around the head of the inlet, I wade carefully across the water channel. It is more suited to wellingtons than walking boots and I struggle across rocks heavily coated with bladder and spiral wrack, arriving on the other side with well-washed boots, socks, and mucky trousers. Two Large White butterflies cruise past as I make my way through fields and clamber over fences before re-emerging on the road at Finavarra. A 3-metre-high memorial to a poet overlooks the bay at Parkmore where orange lichen-covered steps provide a resting place. The pillar stone is in memory of Donncha Mor Ó Daliagh, venerable poet of the thirteenth century. Daisies and buttercups pepper the ground around it. In a field behind me, set on a height, lies the shell of Finavarra House surrounded by silent cows. Part of it is covered with ivy. The whole area was at one time part of the Finavarra estate.

Mist still encloses the higher reaches of the hills but a warming lunchtime sun is emerging to burn it off as I munch my sandwiches. Gulls whirl around in choreographic disorder when I rejoin the coastline. My route turns south and I leave behind the Flaggy Shore where I have made reasonable progress. I recall the parting motto from Mark at Mount Vernon: 'No room for flagging on the Flaggy Shore'. A mix of rock and grassy coastline takes me the next kilometre or so into Bell Harbour. The stones and pebbles are shot through with a variety of colours. I think about how walking empties my mind of thoughts, allowing me to concentrate on the present – the here and now – not what happened last week or what might happen next month. Most of us are rarely alone, but walking on your own is the best way to appreciate scenery because it allows you to tune your senses into the land and seascape.

When I reach Bell Harbour, the clouds have dissolved to give way to columns of sunlight. I pay €3 for a mug of tea and a bar of chocolate in Daly's Corcomroe pub. With a brightly quizzical eye, the barman raises his bushy eyebrows several times at my journey. 'Faith,' he says 'it'll be another damn good three hours along the coast to reach Ballyvock-han.'

The tentacles of development are tightening their grip on Bell Harbour near the small car park and quay. Following roadside hedges wallpapered with red valerian, I make my way down to the shorefront beyond an Ó Lochlainn Tower by a track beside Bell Harbour House where two dogs strain on leads. The sun-spangled afternoon is turning into an oasis of flat calm with a stillness settling over the sea.

I return to my thoughts of being alone when I realise that I have company. More than twenty seals with pups are chilling out *en famille* on the rocks. One or two stand to attention in the water, others frolic around. Although I tread softly, trying not to disturb their dreamy sunny siesta, and conceal myself behind a high wall, some speedily take to the water, peering up at me, bottling with their heads and necks clear of the water. Half-a-dozen others bask gracefully on the seaweed-freckled rocks, sizing me up and staring with inquisitive coal-black eyes at this stranger on their shore. Leaning quietly on top of the wall, I watch them at length. They are at one with the rocks, merging perfectly. Through binoculars, they look overweight and cumbersome, lying with their heads lifted and hind flippers curving into the air. Their colours fascinate me; some are spotty, others are brown, and their wet and shiny coats have blotches. Suddenly, an unseen noise, and in an instant they dive underwater, re-emerging seconds later to come up for air. One snorts harshly, and another sounds as if it is blowing its snout. Some slither back into the water and swim farther out, while others haul themselves back up on to the rocks. Two scratch their fore flippers idly and shuffle around. I have never before seen so many gathered in one spot with their long whiskers so visible.

The Music of the Sea

Making my way along the pavement, I have a feeling that I am being followed. A couple of my aquatic friends tag along in the water for a short distance before one falls by the wayside. The remaining one coughs twice; I cough back, then we cough together. After twenty paces, I look around – dark, quizzical eyes fixed on me. He nods briskly out of the water, bobs several times, and with a cheeky farewell wink, performs a swift underwater disappearing trick returning to playtime with his chums.

Another hour, another tower. The tower at Muckinish West is a partially collapsed one. From the road it looks in sound shape but approaching it from the seafront I discover that its frontage has collapsed, giving it a forlorn appearance. Trees decorate the second storey, and grass, weeds, and flowers colonise its crumbling walls. A potholed path with grass along the centre leads to a sharp corner where the coast swings around to a beach filled with grey stones and shingle from where I look across to the Flaggy Shore. My route rises to grassy coastal cliffs before the terrain quickly turns into a path along sand dunes spangled with gentians. The crisp, soft sand feels gentle on my boots, a relaxing contrast to the cracked limestone. A woman with two dogs pauses on Bishopsquarter beach. As I pass the Whitethorn restaurant and Burren House, the sea takes on a distinctly choppy appearance.

The final stretch of the day takes me into Ballyvaughan, looking deceptively serene for a Friday night. It is 6.15 p.m. and a listless early evening torpor hangs over the village. It will be at least another three hours before the music-makers in the pubs open their fiddle cases and unwrap their tin whistles. A couple of herring gulls pace querulously up and down the waterfront wall. Over a bar meal I read in the paper about the rain and the so-called 'European monsoon' which has swept across Britain and appears to be heading for Ireland. Fortunately the anticipated heavy rain has not yet reached County Clare.

Greene's is a plain-looking pub in the main street with gallowglass military figures on panels outside. With a promising air of musical expectation, the bar fills soon after opening time at 9.00 p.m. Most customers stand at the bar and the few tables and chairs are quickly taken. A two-man group entertains Saturday evening drinkers with 'Will Ye Go Lassie Go' and 'The West's Awake'. The bearded bodhrán player tilts his curly head of hair, snuggling it closely to his instrument. His companion launches into a majestically paced version of 'Nancy Spain'. The bar quietens. With little facial expression he runs through the verses with emotion and passion, every syllable of each word eked out, his eyes gazing fixedly on the window throughout. The poignancy of the song has an electrifying effect on two women standing in front of me. Their eyes moisten and teardrops run down their faces, adding to the mess of their already smudged lip-gloss. A nanosecond before the applause, a grey-haired bewhiskered woman in a grape-green woollen cardigan who had been sitting at the bar on a high stool, twitching her nose throughout the rendition, having small conversations with herself, signals her loud approval: 'Gudman Liam.'

A series of reels quickens the tempo. 'Toss the Feathers', 'The Morning Star' and 'The Bucks of Oranmore' activate some spectators. A tall pony-tailed woman with a long pre-Raphaelite neck and wearing tight jeans gets up to inject her own personality into the entertainment. With remarkable feisty footwork, she pounds the floor, kicking her legs higher and ever higher raising the pulse of the packed house. Two girlfriends frame her movements in the small screen of mobile phone cameras capturing the digital perfection of the moment. Hand-in-hand a German couple performs a stiff and uncertain jig across the cream linoleum kitchen floor, giving up halfway through with warm blushes and embarrassed laughter. Drinkers chortle into their pints. Reminiscent of a Muckinish seal, the bewhiskered woman creases her right eye into a cheerful wink, burps like a windy baby, and whispers to me through yellow teeth 'In here we call that lino dancing.'

Day Three: Saturday 29 May

Over breakfast at the next table in the Mount Vernon dining room, an American couple, on a whirlwind tour of Clare, plan their day's activities.

She: 'So where are we going today?'

He: 'Ennistymon.'

She: 'I thought we were there yesterday.'

He: 'That was Ennis, today it's Ennistymon – a different place.'

She: 'Don't you just love the cute names they all have?'

Ennis had failed to register on the Oregon woman's Richter scale of Irish towns. This is at odds with the story on the front page of *The Clare Champion* under the headline: 'Ennis a world-class tourist destination'. The article was about the fact that Ennis has been named as one of the world's 'great places'. It is on a par with Grand Central Station in New York, Nôtre Dame Cathedral in Paris and the Spanish Steps in Rome.

I drive into Ballyvaughan to start the second stage of my walk, parking on the Black Head road beside a bird hide. With a morning spring in my step, I watch a limpid sun rise slowly in the sky and, passing the hide, decide not to play peekaboo with the birds. I prefer my birds flying rather than laminated, so instead I let them see me flying over the limestone, warbling as I go with my rucksack bouncing on my shoulders, pacing my stride to the beat. My senses are tingling with the rhythm of the sentimental tunes from last night and 'Nancy Spain' plays in my head:

No matter where I wander I'm still haunted by your name.
The portrait of your beauty stays the same.
Standing by the ocean, wondering where you've gone,
If you'll return again . . .

A lone heron in slow flight glides to land as if in appreciation
of my singing. With forensic thoroughness, it picks and wades
carefully through a messy tangle of shingle and seaweed.
Holding its pose on lanky wire-thin legs, it then lifts, blowing
briefly sideways in the wind before a swift gear change allows
it to take off with a quiet ease looking like a miniature bit part
from *Jurassic Park*.

Seen from the coast, the Burren hills have a beguiling
radiance, music-softened (in my head at least) by the ethereal
strains of the night before. The ground is richly decorated with
spring sandwort, sea thrift and burnet rose. Several skylarks are
out and about. A herd of jet-black cows grazes in the sun. Chewing
ruminatively, two horses – a mare and a foal accompanied by a
donkey – stand on a grassy spit of land that looks out to Farthing
Rocks. It is turning into a crystal clear day and the glowing sun
brings out the best in the shiny pewter stones.

An hour's walk across boulder-strewn pavement and
ankle-high grass suffused with bloody cranesbill, early purple
orchids and gentians brings me to the townland of Gleninagh.
Concentrating on the flora, I had not noticed that a billowing
bank of cloud had scudded across the sky. Magpies, skylarks and
two great-black-backed gulls vie in the air space. I step up my
pace, and a brisk twenty-minute walk takes me to a spot where a
high bank falls about 30m from the road. It is an out-of-the-way
little-visited but attractive sheltered spot. Chinaman's hats are
embedded on the jagged, honeycombed rocks. A marine snail,
better known as the common periwinkle, blazes a slow course
along a slime trail. The high sides of the banks are festooned

with a breadcrumb sponge and dripping velvety green moss the colour of Chartreuse liqueur. On a dark, pyramidal rock in the water, a cormorant stands, wings outstretched like a heraldic creature, while two others sail around it, gently riding on the incoming waves.

Just beyond this point I am forced on to the road as the steep, slippery and rocky drop into the sea deters me from trying to negotiate it. The positive effect of ten minutes of tarmac brings a bonus as masses of creamy mountain avens grow profusely along both sides of the road. Four women greet me with wide grins and trekking pole salutes. Hard on the wheels of a tour bus two kamikaze Kawasakis bank around the corner while I cling to the grassy verge holding tight to clumps of *dryas*. The elevation of the road provides a viewing point for gazing down into the sea where I pick out two black guillemots with striking red legs diving for fish and molluscs.

Holding a white and lonely vigil, Black Head lighthouse marks the point where my route swings sharply south. Across the wide expanse of ocean, the Aran Islands are visible. I reflect on Paul Valéry's 'long vistas of celestial calm'. A herd of beefy cows swish tails at me. They watch while I take a nip from my hip flask of Burren 'tea' to round off the 4 inches of baguette I have eaten and help wash my soup down with some authority.

Farther along I come upon a dancing wheatear, glowing in its cinnamon-grey, black and white plumage. Flying low in short spurts, it hops from clint to boulder perching every so often, looking around with a nervous demeanour and a trilling song. I have often been intrigued by its name which has nothing to do with wheat. The white flash above its tail comes from the Anglo-Saxon 'whit-ers', meaning 'white arse.' The bird's name was later bowdlerised to something less offensive.

The afternoon sun is now casting cloud shadows on the hills. Black Head and the area south of it, Murrough, is where the Burren coastline meets the lines of tourists. A couple of red-fleeced and red-faced Dutch visitors ask me to take their photo. It is an area rich in erratics streaked with lichen and intricately detailed drystone walls with exquisite fretwork. I clamber over several walls, dislodging and, swiftly obeying the Burren Code, replacing stones. As I ponder the power of the sea and the fact that these waves have travelled thousands of kilometres, I feel the salt on my lips, skin and hair. A mixed collection of ponies and donkeys graze quietly with a look of dull misery in their eyes. The limestone is part of a Special Area of Conservation with long, smooth, clear stretches of clints and overflowing fern-filled grykes.

After two hours of steady tramping I throw off my rucksack at a sheltered cliff spot and watch the waves in two-metre-high breaks of foamy spray rolling in, then retreating rapidly in swirls. Around the coast small cottages are dotted at intervals. My eye follows the swerve of the coastline towards Fanore still some distance away and the finishing point for today. It is a good place to watch the froth and backwash of the sea and listen to the elemental sounds. Lying on a soft clump of grass, I fall into a contemplative reverie letting the noises drift over me: the relentless suck and surge of powerful waves, the quiet sigh of the wind slipping through the rocks, bees burring, and a raven cawing above me, circling and looking down on the splash zone. This is a place to enjoy the tempestuousness of the sea. Like many parts of the west of Ireland, it is, in the words of Praeger, somewhere 'you can listen to the sea shouting on the rocks'.

Up and down sand dunes filled with marram grass and sea holly, and along a high, narrow clifftop path, the final stretch leads to the wide curving expanse of Fanore beach. A handful of dog walkers cross it; three teenage girls paddle-giggle and then shriek their way out to the dissolving white wave crests. Two hardy body boarders successfully ride the frothing surf. It feels good to walk on floury sand after many hours of pavement, rocks and stones, although much more energy is required to walk on sand, compared to the limestone. My boots sink 5 or 6cm, leaving deep footprints along the strandline. Halfway across, I examine some delicate blue freckled seashells and watch the wave-trains rolling in rhythmically, then intermingling and overtaking each other. Globules of foam break loose on to the beach running along the sand. Two ringed plovers scamper around in circles. Listening carefully, I hear a low whistling across the grains of sand but cannot make out the tune. It sounds as though someone is blowing into a half-filled bottle.

The dune system at Fanore is classified as a European Special Area of Conservation and to protect it Clare County Council has fenced off areas at risk from trampling. Fanore beach, with its rash of attached caravans, marks the final stage of day three, but one further obstacle remains to be surmounted: a wide river flowing down in a temper tantrum across the sand, and running out to sea. The Caher River is several centimetres deep and as I do not want to end my day with wet socks and boots, I remove them and wade across, arms outstretched cormorant-like. I had not expected so much seaweed and stones underfoot, and slip several times before accidentally dropping my boots into the river.

Day Four: Sunday 30 May

Failte go Fanoir says the stone slab (erected by the St Patrick's Day Committee in 2005) as I pull into the car park at the beach under a sky rinsed of cloud. The final stage of my coastal route takes me from Fanore along a lengthy stretch of pavement to Doolin. The Irish Cycling Safari minibus drops off its customers and ten lycra-clad, fat-bottomed bikers prepare to set off on their own Burren exploration.

I follow a rocky staircase that quickly takes me down to the seashore at Craggagh, passing large erratics shaped like rugby balls and small metre-high stone cairns. Unlike the smooth, flat type with neat, rounded angles, the pavement here is pitted and fissured, and has a scarred effect. Walking on the limestone is a delicate art because some clints are not firm, but even greater care is needed on the slippery, shattered pavement. Steps must be carefully placed and although it is hard to find an even gait, I eventually achieve a steady pace. Three schmoozing fishermen enjoy their rock-angling on this sun-spangled morning. From Poll Salach another wide stretch of pavement takes me through stimulating place names that communicate a sharp visual image: Cahermaclanchy, Ballyvoe, Ballycahan and Teergonean.

At Ballyryan a queue has formed at a hot-food bar. With clipboards, sketch pads, paint boxes and picnic baskets, a group of eighteen artists attempts to capture the texture of the rocks and clints on a weekend painting school. Heads down, hands capped behind their backs as though attending a prayer meeting or graveside oration, they listen to their tutor all 'depth of field' and instruction on the intricacies of horizontal dimensions.

Rock pipits dance around playfully and brown butterflies emerge as I make my way back to the seafront where recumbent cows gleam in haughty languor. The walking is now more stable with light scrambling to tackle some higher cliffs. The sea comes into a little cove and foams run up against the cliffs cascading over rocks. Two climbers below me search for handholds. I play a one-sided game of see-saw with an enormously unsteady clint and pause to look up at a giant erratic that looks as if it could topple into the sea at any moment.

I lunch perched on a boulder looking out to the Aran Islands with their low, slightly humped profile. The middle island, Inis Meáin, resembles the shape of an upturned currach. Save for the cry of the gulls and lapping water, there is no noise. Cranesbill, primroses, heath spotted-orchids and banded snails decorate the ground. I have gained some height through climbing and find myself in the company of fulmars. With their stiff wings like airfix model aeroplanes, they glide gracefully, banking, riding effortlessly on the updraught before swooping down. I admire their skilful movements. One treads air for a few seconds, glides close eyeing me suspiciously with a look and a brisk *ack ack ack ack* that I translate as 'Have you permission to be here?' I decide not to advance any nearer to the cliff face because fulmars are known for spurting a foul-smelling oily substance at intruders.

Within minutes, I come to a grassy section filled with scores of bright purple orchids. Standing tall and singly, or in groups of three or four, I attempt a head-count of extended families: 50, 100, then 200 and up to 500 – and although my census is unscientific – I discover a staggering number growing at this secluded spot. Zigzagging up a grassy slope, I negotiate a headland and confront more stone walls. Struggling to get a foothold, I fall back several times. I had come across holes in the walls called sheep creeps and silently wonder as I battled awkwardly over so many, how useful it would be to have a 'walker creep'.

Half an hour across a mix of flat grass and clusters of Polo Mint style limestone brings me to Doolin harbour which has an edge-of-the-world feel. I arrive weather-beaten, stomach-rumbling, salivating and tramped out. Muscle-fatigue from the pavement bashing is setting in. I have collected toe blisters. For the second consecutive day I take off my boots and socks, and dangle my sore feet into the clear and surprisingly warm Atlantic. A sign warns 'Dangerous Bathing'. Necklaces of foamy waves roll in. Two opportunistic black-plumaged jackdaws pick around a fishing box that is the property of Red Sail Exports Ltd. A gentle breeze gathers pace and dark clouds festoon the sky. A solitary heron looks for a fish supper. The goddess of the coast is looking after travellers and the threatened monsoon has not yet reached the west coast. I gaze out to Crab Island with its small stone coastguard hut. The *Jack B* ferry arrives from the Aran Islands efficiently discharging its cargo of rucksacked passengers. Doolin is overrun with backpackers, coach parties fresh from the Cliffs of Moher experience, Aran Island day trippers, and exhausted Dutch and German tourists. A twenty-minute amble along the Shore Road leads into the centre of the village. Apart from having to dodge the tour buses, walking again on the tarmac is a pleasure. The terra of the road is more firma than the pavement.

Doolin Nightcap

As I began my coastal odyssey in a pub, I feel it appropriate for symmetry's sake to round it off in another one. Doolin offers a varied choice with banjo, mandolin, concertina, tin whistle, fiddle, accordion, guitar or any combination of them. The place is deluged with music, cascading out of the downpipes and the guttering, and flowing along the street every night. At weekends there are often two or three separate sessions. *The Rough Guide to Ireland* has described most of the music played in Doolin as 'amplified garbage'.

To test this view, I arrive just in time in Gus O'Conner's (established in 1832, according to a sign over the door), where an early-evening session featuring The Burrenmen is getting underway. Sure enough the music is piped into every room and amplified through large speakers. Three musicians seated around a table in the centre tune up on guitar, accordion and concert flute. A selection of jigs opens the proceedings: 'The Old Grey Goose', 'The Cliffs of Moher' and 'Spot the Wallop'. Four New Englanders beside me, weighed down with craft and knitwear bags, applaud politely. Both couples are celebrating their ruby wedding anniversaries and clink thin-stemmed Irish coffee glasses. They discuss going for a 'peet-sa' but decide to stay and enjoy the music.

The Burrenmen have lost their lead singer, Tom, owing to a Sunday afternoon alcohol over-indulgence. He hangs his head silently, then opens one eye and closes it quickly. Several times his head tilts back before slumping sideways. Suddenly he wakes with a start, looking around, taking a gulp of beer and nodding off again. A petite blonde comes up to him, punching his stomach.

'Open your eyes,' she shouts several times. 'Tom . . . Tom . . . open your voice box and give us a song.'

The bearded accordion player slaps Tom on the thigh and shouts: 'We're gonna dedicate this next reel to you – "The Teetotaller's Fancy".'

The Americans burst into laughter. One of them, Dick, whispers loudly to his wife, 'I think he's had too much strong licker.'

Dick is having such fun he decides to phone his friend in Boston to make him jealous. His wife shoots him a thirty-year weary glance.

'Hey Joe, Kay-ad Mayllion Failties to you – that's a million welcomes in Irish. You should get over here quick. We're in Toolin in Kerry . . . fact it's called O'Callaghan's Bar and this is where the action is.'

'Doolin,' the barman shouts, frowning at his geographical stupidity and foaming at the mouth, 'and it's in CLARE.' Then, *sotto voce*, 'D for dickhead and we've a right one here. And it's been O'Conner's for a hundred-and-sixty-four bleedin' years.'

The Burrenmen take a break. I pore over the map retracing the route of my energising journey. The infinite variety of terrain included limestone, grassland, tarmac, beach, sand dunes, walls, rocks, stones and pebbles. The sea is an integral part of life here. I had spent long hours and days walking alone with the sea as my only company, its daily dramas the perfect distraction. As I look back on my journey along the Burren littoral and its headlands, I ponder some valedictory thoughts about the history, flowers and animals. Reflecting on the highlights, I think of how the land and sea, shaped by the forces of nature, fit jigsaw-like together. In my mind, I freeze-frame memorable moments: the playful seal colony gathered in a watery *corps de ballet* at Muckinish, the wheatears and rock pipits that accompanied me, the aerial display of the fulmar, and the slow movement of the mist. Add to this the lilt of the New Quay concertinistas, the bewitching beauty of the Ballyvaughan songsters, and The Burrenmen minus their songster.

These are amongst the sweetest sounds: the music of what happened, the sensation of being alive to small events. Raising my glass, I drink a symbolic toast to Our Lady of the Fertile Rock and to my American friends' marital longevity. Through the crowded atmosphere, a selection of reels reignites interest. 'The Maids of Holywell' and 'The Duke of Leinster' flow from the group's table. Sadly there are no songs. The lyrics to The Burrenmen's folk tunes are unsung. As I have discovered, though, music runs through the veins of Clare men and women, a permanent soundtrack to their lives, but the coast itself has been my songline – the crash of the waves, the siren call of the wind, the whistling sand, the gulls' cry, the happy clunk of the clints have all been a part of the intermingling of landscape and music. 'Come West Along the Road' brings my journey to a fitting conclusion as I mull over a strenuous and melodious weekend tuning into *ceol na mara*, 'the music of the sea'.

The Flaggy Shore © Trevor Ferris

12

The Burren Painters

Those who dwell among the beauties and mysteries of the
earth are never alone or weary of life.

Rachel Carson, *The Sea Around Us*

From Donegal to Cork, the west coast of Ireland is a place
of wild seas, magnificent scenery, and dramatic cliffs and
rocks. Since the seventeenth century, landscape painters have
been drawn irresistibly to it for the majesty and pageantry of
its western skies, the dreamy silences, the grandiloquence of
the light and its air of mystery. They have captured the terrain
in its textual and tonal quality. Some of Ireland's best-known
painters such as Alexander Williams, Paul Henry and Charles
Lamb preferred the set pieces of Killary Harbour, Achill Island
or Connemara with its dramatic mountain ranges where they
adopted a technique of what become known as 'simple elegance'.

Other painters, including John Luke with his precise stylised
technique, settled for Mayo. Sligo shaped the artistic vision of
Jack B. Yeats. Some chose the hills of Donegal to produce their
sweeping brushstrokes of clouds and luminous skies and many

picked Killarney with its fusion of mountains and lakes. This distinctive Irish school of painting that included James Humbert Craig alluded to the romantic idealism of the west of Ireland which provided a powerful stimulus for their imagination. In their vast canvases there is a strong feeling of light, air and spaciousness, and many of their works have a sense of stillness as well as a feeling of wildness and loneliness. Some made their homes and reputations in the west, filling their sketchbooks and producing memorable works of artistic gravitas.

With their lower profile, the Burren hills lack the iconographic picturesqueness, triangular symmetry and drama of some of Clare's neighbours that are associated with the west. They are on a smaller, less exalted, mountain scale. There are few rivers to paint and no tumbling waterfalls or romantic lakes for artists to give an imaginative response to or with which to flirt; yet the physical landscape makes a striking first impact. It has enticed painters of different outlooks and techniques for the constantly changing sky and seascapes, the towering cloudscapes, the world of moving shadows across the hills and fresh minted landscape brought about by the weather patterns. There is so much scope with the southern shore of Galway Bay and a scenic maze of islands, headlands, tidal creeks and sandy bays just a bravura brush stroke away.

In terms of the landscape, little has changed in hundreds of years. This is partly the attraction for the painter. The visual and aesthetic value is strong. The dynamic light is much as it always was. The painters who come to the Burren are enchanted by the crystal clear light shining through the clouds, the exciting atmospheric conditions, and the expanse of sea and sky together with the vaporous mist. They also love the overwhelming sense of peace and distilled calm. The skies in particular are a material part of their work and a keynote element. More than anywhere else in the west, painters here get a lot of sky for their money.

It is a stunning landscape to enliven their compositions. It has an emotive power: stimulating, strong, savage and often primitive. There is an agelessness and timelessness through the antiquity of the stones and the walls that appeals to their painterly eyes. The dancing waves are another attraction. The Burren is underpopulated and unspoilt by industrialisation. There are no huge housing developments, no sprawling estates on the edges of its towns. The exposed limestone gives it character and liveliness. It is what many look for when painting and seeps deep into their consciousness. The greyness pervades their work and is inherent in many of their landscapes.

Although it is a place that is high on the emotional radar of artists, it does not lend itself to as figurative an approach as other western shores. The Burren eludes some of them; they pack their bags and quickly move on. Not all painters find that emotional instant effect. They have difficulty capturing the actuality of it, engaging with or interpreting its mood, so they settle elsewhere for what they see as more pleasing vistas. It is no place for the realist painter. Some of those who visit it are not receptive to its strange atmosphere. There are no bogs or people leading donkeys with peat-filled panniers across fields. So much of the visual representation of the west of Ireland's rural landscape has produced cliché and stereotype but the Burren's romantic glamour of indistinctness is not to everyone's taste.

Over the years it has nonetheless attracted the imaginative energy of artists of the calibre of Robert Gregory (the subject of W. B. Yeats' poem 'An Irish Airman Foresees his Death'), Barrie Cooke, Anne Madden, Brian Bourke, and the Donegal-based painter Derek Hill who died in July 2000. They developed a liking for the region, spending in some cases a considerable amount of time in the area and the Burren became an important location in their work. Some adopted a light touch in their portrayal of the rock and limestone hills; others produced work redolent of a poetic style with an apparent calmness, while a few chose to explore with vibrant colours and free brush strokes.

~~~

In the brightly lit attic of his house hidden down an alleyway in Ballyvaughan, Manus Walsh is surrounded by scores of examples of his artwork – some complete, others half-finished, and a few at the artistic incubation stage. When he first came to New Quay on the Flaggy Shore in the summer of 1975 Manus was immediately captivated by the mystery of the Burren. Its uniqueness appealed to him, allied to the fact that it was completely different to anywhere else that he had been. The challenge was to capture, through his imagination, its forbidding and lonely nature.

He settled in Ballyvaughan in 1976 and since then has painted the Burren from every conceivable angle, tapping into its rhythms and moods. As he walks the roads his eyes are attuned to small details and odd shapes that he sees and then sketches: an isolated tree or peculiar boulder, the horizontal line of a stone wall, or a turlough, are all scenes that might normally be overlooked.

'At the start I didn't know anything about the place,' he admits over a coffee. 'But I was a good walker and used to go into the Wicklow Mountains nearly every weekend. So when I came down here I began exploring it. I just took to it and its different lights, although it did take a while as I was immersed in setting up an enamelling business. I went out with my binoculars, sketchbook and flask of tea and walked every inch of the place. Living here all the time with kids, I just fell in love with it. I took up cycling and got to know the back roads which are a great way to see and feel the place. The traffic gets heavy in the summer but when you know the quiet roads such as the

Caher Valley, it's easier to stop and take in the landscape.'

Manus is a multi-talented artist who is self-taught. He uses acrylics, collages, oils, watercolours, gouache, chalk and glass. Worktables in his studio are crammed with jars of burnt umber and burnt sienna, yellow ochre, cobalt blue, ultramarine, Payne's grey, Naples deep yellow and sap green. He talks about the evolution of his paintings and his technique.

'Every time I sit down with a blank piece of paper I tend to find that my work unravels as I go along. A few times, of course, it doesn't work out but the great thing about acrylics is that you can go over it straightaway. I've come to the end of paintings sometimes and said to myself this isn't working and I start again and over-paint, which lots of painters do. So it evolves on the canvas or the paper. The collages are the black and white ones, which are quite dramatic. I go back to them from time to time as it's a new way of showing the landscape. I am very aware of the colours all the time and my main ones are greens, browns and saffron.'

With their shadowy blurs and cloud-filled skies, his paintings have a melodramatic impact with long views, close-ups, or moonlit night. You have to look closely into his work to see what is there. Like many good paintings the longer you look at them the more you see. But Manus does not attempt a precise reproduction of the landscape and is not aiming for an accurate topographical view. In keeping with the spirit of the place, the result is a style that he calls 'semi-abstract impressionism'. His work reflects the stark, stratified nature of the hills at night and he has produced a series on the lunar landscape – the Burren moon – which has become a staple theme and crucial part of his pictorial architecture.

'The moon features quite a lot in my work because it is so dramatic especially over Moneen and Aillwee mountains where it looks huge. I often laugh because people say it's like a Hollywood moon. It seems as though someone is behind the mountain pulling it up like a hydraulic moon or sometimes it even looks as if it's on a piece of string. The moon is a focal point in the painting shining on the turloughs which helps bring the viewer into the work.

'There is drama in the Burren with the moon and on bright nights the rocks become silvered. There are so many moods but when you are up close it's quite hard to capture it because it's almost abstract already with the rock shape. You could go crazy trying to capture it but it's the rhythm of the landscape I try to portray. I come back and go straight into the acrylics because I find them immediate while the other drying agents take a good deal of time to dry. I also use quite a stiff brush for the acrylics which helps.'

One of the important aspects of a painter's life, he says, is to be ready for sudden movements in the weather. The incessant changes in the light and moods have to be caught – whether it is the sheen on the limestone after rain, the glittering sun, the half, or crescent, moon. Like a chef, he gathers his ingredients, mixing them bit by bit in dabs and splashes on to his canvas cooking up a visual alchemy and stirring his creative spirit. From his palette he creates, by a synthesis of different elements, the overall feeling rather than a specific place. Never simply accepting what is there, he makes up his own skies.

'The light is one of the key things and trying to capture that is an ongoing battle. The changes of light are amazing as the hills turn pink and purple. I remember the poet John O'Donohue stopping me in the middle of the street about six months before he died in 2008. He said that he'd seen my paintings and was amazed as he never thought there was blue in the Burren. He was really taken by that aspect of the blueness which is not very obvious. The colours are seasonal with the tan and saffron in the winter. In June the ground gets burnt with the hot weather.'

Burren Country

It is, he concedes, a challenging place to interpret, which is the reason why many painters do not stay long. Manus has produced a series of landscapes with horizontal lines, full of ghosts and often devoid of colour.

'It certainly is a difficult landscape to interpret and you have to be here a long time to try to get underneath the skin of it. It looks barren with the rocks but if you look in between then it's quite fertile with trees and bushes, which make it almost abstract already with those tortured shapes. Seascapes are straightforward because it's a rocky coast but when you get into the interior with the terracing it's harder.'

We walk around his house and he shows me his framed paintings hanging on walls. 'You can see in this Burren one that I do a kind of stippling effect which gives the rhythm of the rocks and walls. It brings liveliness to the painting with blue skies and spots of green. I start a number of paintings at the same time, then leave one aside and come back to it. I put it down on the floor and have a look at it later so it goes in layers and I could go back to it five or six times before I get the finished piece.'

I ask about specific locations in his work but he mostly does not put place names in the title. They tend to be generic with such titles as 'Burren Pastures', 'Black Night, Misty Burren', 'Burren Green & Grey', or 'Turlough Behind the Hill'.

'Most times it's not an exact place, just my own interpretation rather than the particular. I could put names on the titles but I don't – it wouldn't be factual as they aren't specific places so it would be incorrect to call them, for example, Mullaghmore or Moneen. Tom Kenny in Galway laughs at me and says you'll have to come up with some new titles such as 'Burren in the morning', 'Burren in the evening', 'Burren at summer time' . . . so getting a name that alludes to the landscape in its different moods is difficult. Even people who know the Burren well couldn't identify the locations. They like to have a name sometimes if it's a particular painting that they like and they ask: "Do I know this place? Is that up the back of Gleninsheen?" I like keeping them guessing.'

Manus looks perplexed when I ask about the number of paintings he has done of the Burren and seems to have lost count. 'I've never kept a record and it's hard to quantify it but I've been exhibiting for more than thirty-four years.'

His first one man show was in Dublin in 1967. We calculate that he has produced at least 700 Burren paintings, perhaps even more than this. In 2010, when he was seventy, he held a major exhibition 'As I Walked Out' in Kenny's Gallery.

'You try to do your very best for each one and set yourself a standard, hoping that people will say this is your best exhibition yet. It's a personal thing as I'm not thinking of anything else but the painting at the time that I'm working on as it's very absorbing. Some people who follow my exhibitions say there's a lot more colour in recent years, so they've seen a progression but I mightn't notice it myself. I think most artists get more skilful over the years as it is a craft to be learned using the materials to suit your needs.'

Manus' favourite Burren location is Bishopsquarter beach which for him has a tranquil feel. 'There are tremendous contrasts in the place in the summer and winter. I used to swim at Bishopsquarter every evening and it is highly atmospheric. I love the peace of it off season, and especially when you get the sun it is a quiet place until the Brent geese arrive in the autumn. When I'm on my bike I like to get a good cycle up Ballyallaban hill, or around Black Head, up the Caher Valley or down to Carron. It is a great mixture.'

Like much of the work of west of Ireland painters, there is a stillness and pellucid softness about his Burren canvases. But as a contrast, Manus has also painted abroad. He has spent time in Spain, Cuba, France, Morocco and Chile and this experience has had a deep effect on his work, producing an infusion of a dance of colours. His Galway exhibition included work from Chile and Spain, as well from the souks of the Moroccan towns of Tétouan and Chefchaouen. Tétouan is a whitewashed town hidden between the Mediterranean and the Rif region. Largely forgotten by tourists, it was once the makeshift capital of Spanish Morocco and, along with Chefchaouen, has provided Manus with new vistas to produce eye-catching watercolours.

'I've been going to Spain since 2001 although it all goes back to the days of George Campbell who was my mentor in the 1960s and was a huge influence on my work. He was from Arklow and later went to live in Belfast. I met him through my stained-glass work and he encouraged me to come to Spain so I went out and stayed for a couple of months with him. Ever since then I've kept up that relationship with Spain. I go there in the winter to get away from the severity of the weather here. It's a question of moving from the rocks to the olives which you find there in the huge Andalusian fields and it is an amazing difference.

'What I enjoy is the total contrast with the Burren. In Valparaiso I painted cityscapes and the white villages of Spain. These are totally different colours and the light too is a great change. People said it brought more colour to my work here although I wouldn't really notice it but maybe your mood lifts with the stronger sun and brighter days. One of the big differences is the fact that in the Burren the landscape I paint is horizontal with the terraces and stone walls as it is a stratified landscape whereas in Spain it is vertical.'

Manus points out several of his Valparaiso works hanging on his walls which have an exuberance not found in his Burren paintings and which in some cases embrace the fiery end of the red-orange colour spectrum. His Spanish artwork is populated with figures while his Burren works are mostly, but not always, bereft of people.

In his early days working in stained glass he produced five windows in Galway Cathedral and in 2003 made a much-loved memorial window dedicated to Michael Green in St John the Baptist Church in Ballyvaughan. Manus comes from an artistic pedigree. His grandfather was the novelist and short story writer Maurice Walsh who was born at Ballydonoghue near Listowel in County Kerry in 1879. He worked for Customs and Excise in 1901, serving mostly in the Scottish highlands which gave him the settings for many stories. In 1922 he transferred to the Irish customs service in Dublin and began his fiction.

'I was in my teens and early twenties when he was writing and he was very encouraging to me as I was artistic and played music. He had a particular grá or liking for me.'

Before I leave, Manus shows me a collection of his grandfather's books on his shelves that include hardback first editions in dust wrappers as well as paperbacks. Unlike his grandson, he did give specific titles to his work although there are nomenclatural echoes of Manus' paintings in some: *While Rivers Run*, *Danger Under the Moon* and *Green Rushes* which contains 'The Quiet Man' story on which John Ford based his famous film in 1952.

'The novels have been reprinted and have been out of fashion a bit but he wrote some very good books. He had a prolific output of adventure stories often with historical settings and his writing pleased millions of readers in Ireland, Britain and the United States.'

In a different artistic medium, Manus' work too is constantly sought after and is in private collections in many countries around the world. And even after thirty-five years of prolonged exposure to the limestone along with quiet and contemplative exploration of the rhythms of the Burren's back roads and hideaways, he still finds new themes and subjects to paint.

'I suppose there is a danger that you could run out of ideas here and you could become bogged down as a Burren painter but I have done quite a bit of work abroad which keeps it fresh. I brought up my family here and at the time I fell into it and it became my home. Even though I was born and bred in Stillorgan, I have no inclination ever to go back to Dublin.'

Artist Manus Walsh at his home in Ballyvaughan © Trevor Ferris

~~~

For forty years a Belfast artist had a love affair with the Burren. Raymond Piper, who died in July 2007, had a long association with County Clare and was a regular visitor. As a young boy he developed an interest in natural history after moving with his family from London to Belfast.

He got to know Clare and its back roads while working on illustrations for Richard Hayward's book *Munster and the City of Cork* (published in 1964). Piper produced more than 120 evocative sketches of the built heritage, landscape and street scenes. The book includes a two-page spread of his delicate line drawings of the Burren flora featuring geraniums, wild strawberry, mountain avens and burnet rose. He also sketched some of the area's best-known antiquities such as the Poulnabrone dolmen, Leamaneh Castle, the High Cross at Kilfenora, the Crucifixion and Sheela-na-Gig at Kilnaboy Old Church, and the double-headed Tau Cross at Kilnaboy.

The two men travelled thousands of kilometres around Ireland and Hayward's infectious enthusiasm rubbed off on Piper who became interested not only in the wild flowers, but also in archaeology and geology. Writing about the Burren, Hayward described it as 'a region of unearthly bare limestone hills like some displaced section of the moon'. Together they walked the roads and pavement, seeking out information from local people when they could find them. Hayward wrote about how they spent four hours at Carron exploring the area and coming upon a tiny colony of the Irish orchid (*Neotinea intacta*) 'wasting its very real beauty on the desert air . . . where we never met or saw a living soul'.

On their Clare rambles they also spent time in Ennis, Quin, Newmarket-on-Fergus, Killaloe, and visited Bunratty Castle. But it was the Burren that enchanted Piper. His journey in the

Raymond Piper at his home in Belfast

company of Hayward added a new dimension to his life. It was the start of a love affair with the place that saw him return on numerous annual pilgrimages to quarter the ground in search of wild flowers. Over the next four decades it would become a happy hunting ground for his botanising. With precision and intricate detail he drew all the species of the exquisite orchids and their variants.

In 1967 Piper was staying in the Falls Hotel in Ennistymon when he met a Dublin photographer, Dick Deegan, and an Irish botanist, George McLean. He had little or no knowledge of orchids or their habitats but wanted to find the dense-flowered orchid and so they set off into the heart of the Burren in search of it. With childlike wonder and astonishment Piper saw orchids everywhere – in marshy fields, on roadside verges and banks, and near houses. Within a short space of time they found not only the dense-flowered orchid, but also the fly orchid, bee orchid, fragrant orchid, early purple, and common spotted orchids all growing in proliferation. This marked the start of a fanatical interest in these attractive and ostentatious flowers, and an insatiable demand for knowledge. He had a gravitational pull towards the area around Ballyvaughan and went on to discover many secret places.

Visitors to his home in Belfast who expressed an interest in Clare would be treated to a detailed run down of the flora sites. Unfurling his copy of the Folding Landscapes map, he delighted in pointing out places he knew well from his field trips, and a torrent of townland names would pour forth: Boston, Lough Bunny, Mullaghmore, Corcomroe, Eagle's Rock, Cahermacnaghten and Rinnamona as well as the coast road around Black Head down to Aill an Daill and Poll Salach. Like a London taxi driver, he had 'the knowledge' borne of years of experience and knew where to go and when to go. He could direct friends on a quest for the gentian, common butterwort, or hoary rockrose to specific sites whether it was via a boreen, near the location of a particular giant erratic or beside a ruined church.

As a self-taught botanist he followed in the illustrious footsteps of Praeger. One of the most thumbed books in his collection which became his vade mecum was Praeger's *A Tourist's Flora of the West of Ireland*, first published in 1909. Piper became a champion of the Burren and was lured back to it regularly. In 1968 he painted a suite of wild flowers that included mountain avens, twayblade, gentian and wild strawberry in oil on prepared boards. His original orchid drawings now hang, framed and protected under glass, in the sitting room of the secluded Gregan's Castle Hotel.

During the 1990s he was involved in the controversial campaign against the proposed building of the Mullaghmore interpretative centre, an area he loved with a passion and somewhere he frequently visited. He vigorously supported the Burren Action Group in its determination to overthrow the plans. He was worried about the consequences of the implementation of the project and wrote letters lobbying support from interest groups. After a visit in 1991 he wrote about what he called the 'brutal destruction' of some of the verges on the road from Kilnaboy to Boston:

> Bulldozers have ruthlessly ploughed through banks and verges and heaped the remains of plants, soil and rocks on to the adjacent ground which contained small but important sites. If this debris remains for long the plants covered will not survive. The increasing violation and erosion of the Burren which has taken place deeply concerns me and must be drastically curtailed. Once such a sensitive environment is breached the consequences would be dire and the area concerned would never recover.

Raymond Piper studied orchids, not just for painting, but for conservation reasons because he feared they were dying out. Some orchids are sensitive to environmental change and damage as their roots store food and the current year's leaves provides sustenance for the development of the following years' plants. As long ago as April 1971 – after an Easter survey of the Burren flora – he expressed concern in an interview with *The Clare Champion* about the use of artificial fertilisers by farmers which he claimed had resulted in the killing off of some wild flowers. In later years he became alarmed about the gradual decimation of orchid populations lamenting that no one would listen to him.

Through regular trips, he got to know local people, and from Lisdoonvarna to Ballyvaughan made long-standing friendships. Many found him stimulating company. The poet Michael Longley, who visited the area with him, wrote: 'Walking with him in the Burren was a revelation. I learned more in a morning or an afternoon with him than I would have learned in a year. He gave me some of the most fulfilling and unclouded times of my life.'

He was a man who knew the colours, feel and texture of the landscape and its flowers intimately. For the painter of the Burren flora, he used to say, the secret is all about mixing tones. Capturing their true colour involves a mixture of tints of all the vast range of shades available on the artists' chart. In his orchid painting he used two predominant colours: brilliant purple No. 1 and oxide of chromium green.

'The chromium green is a versatile medium green and works well with other colours such as yellow ochre, Indian red, rose madder, white and blue,' he said. 'Like the grey of the limestone, the greens vary enormously with a motley selection.'

He once told me that he used what he described as 'thump happy' colours. 'These,' he said, 'are dark, neutral shades, the strong, tough old stalwarts of brown and black which add a final flourish.'

I made a list of the names of the oil colours on the squeezed tubes of paint lying on tables and on chairs in his studio: cerulean blue, lemon yellow, ultramarine, cadmium yellow, alizarin, flesh tint, crimson lake, Prussian green, winsor blue, transparent gold ochre, Vandyke brown, cinnabar.

The most basic colour he used was a neutral tint which he described as a deep grey, neither black nor white but with a hint of blue in it. He used it for painting white flowers, for toning them and for shadows. One of the most brilliant colours for him was cadmium lemon pale, a brilliant yellow which is necessary for highlights and leaves, and other parts of the flower. Capturing the true colour to make an exact reproduction of the magical quality of these fragile flowers on to his watercolour absorbing paper is not easy.

'It's like playing the piano with different keys and choosing your own colour. It is all down to observation and experimenting through many years of experience. Sometimes it may look garish and you have to tone it in, but you can't see colours in isolation. The light is vitally important because it reflects on the flowers.'

He used risky colours with many subtleties of form. To get the exactitude takes time. For the gentian he used ultramarine and cerulean, adding a dash of quinacridone. Apart from the paint tubes littering every space, his cluttered studio was full of jars with sets of brushes, some made from the finest hogs' hair and with long, ivory-coloured, polished handles: thin brushes, flat brushes, fan brushes, watercolour brushes. The length of the bristles was also important to him.

'A longer bristle length gives greater colour-carrying capacity,' he said as he stood back to survey his handiwork. 'But of course you need the shorter bristle too for greater control, delicacy and accuracy and some of them are made to a very fine specification.'

Mrs Puss, Ballyvaughan's famed tortoiseshell cat,
prepares to read about the day's sensations © Trevor Ferris

Drystone wall at Murroughtoohy South © Trevor Ferris

An erratic perch for Paul Clements © Trevor Ferris

Poulnabrone sunset with whitethorn tree © Marty Johnston

Piper's amazement with orchids never left him. His devotion to the subject was total. He gazed on them for many years and for him they were exotic and mysterious. His forty years of singular fascination with the Burren was apparent to all who knew him and his understanding of the diversity of Irish wild orchids was unrivalled. He had a unique awareness of the range of variation within each species, enjoying their exotic nature, the nuances of colour, their charisma and enigmatic scent. His studies of the subject were exhibited in the natural history section of the British Museum.

At the time of his death he was working on a book about the wild orchids of Ireland. He had crafted more than 200 drawings including numerous subspecies and varieties, not just from the Burren, but from other parts of the country. In 1974 he had been awarded the John Lindley medal of the Royal Horticultural Society and elected a Fellow of the Linnean Society of London. Part of the spark that ignited his interest leading to many honours as well as an international reputation was due in no small measure to his love for one area of County Clare which was to always hold a special affection in his heart.

Raymond Piper was well over six feet tall. He had a warm personality and lived life to the full. He enjoyed mimicking people and would often perform with fine oratorical flourishes, grinning all over, with arms waving. He cast a long shadow over the Burren. The orchids have outlived him, but his work will live on in Keelhilla, on Mullaghmore Mountain, along the Flaggy Shore, on Corkscrew Hill, and in the hundreds of other places where he left his flamboyant imprint.

13

Benign Storyteller

Landscape and I get on together well.
Though I'm the talkative one, still he can tell
His symptoms of being to me, the way a shell
Murmurs of oceans.

Norman MacCaig, 'Landscape and I'

When he was a teenager in the late 1960s, Ré Ó Laighléis
cycled from Dublin all the way to the Burren in one day
and had the sorest backside in Ireland. It was an early if painful
encounter with a place that, many years later, would become his
home and the inspirational centrepiece of his creative life.

As well as writing adult fiction, Ré also writes for teenagers
and younger children in both English and Irish. His novels and
short stories have been translated into a variety of languages and
he has won many literary awards. Constantly in demand for
lectures, talks and workshops, he is a versatile and popular writer
whose work has been critically acclaimed.

The Burren's history has penetrated his fantasy fiction
and other stories, many with allegorical and satirical streams.

A Dubliner by birth, he was born in 1953 and brought up in Sallynoggin. Since the 1980s he has adopted the west of Ireland as his home. Bubbling with ideas, Ré has a good-natured personality and, no matter how busy he is, always has time for people. He has given over part of the morning of a day packed with a hectic schedule of radio interviews, meetings and writing, to talk to me at his home near a lake on the outskirts of Ballyvaughan.

As though indelibly imprinted on his mind, he recalls clearly his first trip to the Burren and that memorable bike ride. 'My backside was certainly aching,' he laughs, 'although I was a fit young lad and remained fit into my forties but on that journey I was mindful of all the towns I'd only ever heard of up until then. At home we'd never had a car and never ventured out anywhere as we didn't have the wherewithal. I started seeing these towns and learning their names and they infused in me a great interest in seeing Ireland.'

Ré moved to Galway to teach in the 1980s, frequently visiting the Burren for half-day walks, tramping all over the limestone, inhaling its mystery, listening to its heartbeat and getting to know its secrets. 'There was a strange infusion going on in those walks and seeds were being planted that I never thought were there at all,' he says.

In autumn 1992 he took a career break from teaching and moved to live temporarily in the Burren. This extended to a second, third and fourth year until he decided to pack in teaching and become a full-time writer living near Lough Rask. After four years he gave up the cottage, moved 200m along a narrow boreen and built his own house. He now has a separate writing room, *An Scríobhlann*, a custom-built centre used for training prospective short-story and fiction writers.

From his house, the views take in a triplet of enchanting Burren hills sheltering his cottage: the craggy Aillwee Mountain, the majestic *Sliabh na gCapall* 'the mountain of the horses' and in between them Móinín Mountain beside *Mám Chatha* 'the pass of the battle'. Behind lies the fertile valley of Móinín, a word which translates from the Irish as 'little grassy patch' and is the eponymous name of the publishing company Ré also runs.

One November night, shortly after arriving, he experienced his Burren epiphany when he was awestruck by a partial eclipse of the moon over the hills. 'I went out to the back of the cottage I was renting and watched the totality of the partial eclipse. It might have taken a couple of hours but it was a crystal clear night and I was looking out at Móinín Mountain behind the cottage. The Burren was awash with light and it was a fantastic sight.

'Lots of Burren-related things had happened to me in the previous thirty years and they started running together in a peculiar way. It was like being on some strange substance but the physicality of the place, the flora, and the quality of the landscape all pulled together. I came back in and sat down at my simple little computer and started banging out a story that I had never even thought of previously. I sat for thirty-two hours which was the longest sitting I'd ever done – even longer than the bike ride – with nothing to interrupt me, and I just wrote and wrote.'

At the end of those thirty-two hours Ré had completed four chapters of his novel *Terror on the Burren* (published in 1998). The book is a mix of the supernatural and realism reflecting contemporary events in the Burren including the controversial building of an interpretative centre at Mullaghmore.

'I didn't even sense there was anything allegorical going on between what I was writing and the whole destructive movement concerning the sacred mountain of Mullaghmore. It was only after I'd written it that I realised that what was going on was an influence too. It was an amazing experience. I went to bed and after five hours got up and started into it again. In another four weeks the book was written. So it was definitely an epiphany which was marked very much by suddenness and the unexpected, and all because I had no notion of writing a book.'

Since that moment, there's no doubting the huge impact the area has had on his work. Apart from his Burren fiction, Ré is known for hard-edged contemporary stories. 'Even though I write books that people may think are not in any way Burren-related, living here has enabled me to produce them. It's the freedom it has given me and the sense of place although my books such as *Punk* or *Ecstasy* obviously have nothing to do with the place. They are mainly city-related books but the writing of them has been facilitated by living here.'

His novel *Hooked*, first published in 1999, is the frightening story of a teenage boy's slide into drug addiction and his involvement with a murky and dangerous underworld. The book, filled with the expressive and colourful language of the city streets, also tells the parents' story and how his mother's world is thrown into turmoil.

Heart of Burren Stone (2002) is a collection of twenty short stories, some of which are concentrated on the Burren. Most are based in Ireland, several are set in America, a few in England and one in France. Ré says what has enabled the writing of them has been living in the Burren. When he's not sitting at his computer, he spends a considerable amount of time on the road, leading writing workshops and working with teachers all over Ireland as well as in Britain, Europe and the US. His literary and teaching portfolio has wide parameters; he helps schools with readings and talks under the Poetry Ireland 'Writers in Schools Scheme'. He also conducts training for writers under the Foras na Gaeilge *Scéim na nOidí* (mentoring scheme). In between all this he directs some of his energy into Móinín, a company that publishes children's, teenage and adult fiction in English and Irish.

'Now my life has got much more divided. In a way it's a two-edged sword. The epiphany happened, there was this effluence of work but the result of that is that people want to meet you and this is a delight but the travel element doesn't really have any great pleasure for me now. When you are there you are working and even if it's abroad you don't get to see anything.'

Quickly his conversation returns to the Burren, sparking off a stream of ideas and thoughts. The careful words he chooses flow in an unstoppable, eloquent effusion and his answers often come with a meandering story accompanied by shafts of dry humour. I had heard Ré speak publicly several times and noted his remarkable ability to startle an audience. Punctuated by theatrical gestures and an infectious enthusiasm for his subject, his talks are energised with pure drama: 'It's ROCK . . . ROCK . . . ROCK . . .' he declares, to explain the Burren to outsiders, or sometimes locals who somehow had missed the point of it. He doesn't need any prompting to pick up this theme.

'The rock is magical and everything is in the rock for me because I don't know very much about the flora or fauna, but the rock engages me and what's done with rock in its natural state – the tombs, the dolmens, the cairns, the walls – all those things factor into the rock in so many ways. In *Heart of Burren Stone* I realise how much has gone into it that I hadn't thought of and the best inspiration is osmotic. But encounters with people, the landscape and the sense of something supernatural about it, is what gels and has occasioned my writing. Even for all the age groups I write for, I can't say that any of the books aren't the result of living here.'

Historical fiction is a popular literary genre and Ré has successfully tapped into it. *Battle for the Burren* (2007) is based in Corcomroe Abbey not far from where he lives. 'I decided that as I was into the area of historical record that correctitude might demand that I know what I'm saying so one summer I spent three months researching and note-taking in the National Library, finding out the details of the battle at Corcomroe and surrounding battles. Eventually I read so much I was getting increasingly confused but I was also getting a sense of the historical. I decided I couldn't actually write the book at that point, but something was going on in my head and I went back to the notes. I felt a slave to them so I put down my pen and left it for perhaps two or three years. I was frustrated but felt the best way to do it was to abandon all accurate historical knowledge and write it as a piece of fiction, having the backdrop of the historical knowledge and so I gave up the notes and never went near them again.'

Having abandoned them and created in his subconscious some characters, Ré had found the historical backdrop and did not have to be a slave to accuracy. 'I think that would have allowed the historical to dictate what should be a work of fiction. So I didn't waste my time in the library as I favour being the creator of the information and of how it is presented. And even though I felt I was being a slave, somehow it feeds into the whole, and the strange thing is you don't know ever where a book goes.'

Ré enjoys sharing his skills, knowledge and experience with fledgling writers who are developing their style and trying to find their voice. Nurturing writing talent is part of what he does so encouragingly. 'I often say fiction is fact with a superimposition of the imagination and I think that's as near as I can get to what it is. I meet a lot of adults and teenagers who read my books and it's gratifying that the feedback is amazingly positive. I get more feedback about my contemporary material than my Burren writing but people love to know where a character comes from. And even though I would never portray a person I know as a character in any Burren book, obviously the encounters you have in life attune you to particular types of people.'

His influences stretch back to school and several teachers who were hugely important. 'One was an Irish teacher in Glasthule in Dublin. He was from the Beara peninsula and a very wise man. I don't think he was the greatest teacher of his subject but he was one of the greatest teachers of life. His name was Seán Ó Súilleabháin and he would roll out pearls of wisdom and had a tremendous reflective capacity.'

All this helped Ré create Brother Benignus, an old, blind monk in *Battle for the Burren* who is the re-embodiment of Sobharthan from *Terror on the Burren*. Benignus is an elder of the community of Cistercians in Corcomroe and his name comes from 'benign', the Latin for kindness although in the best tradition of character-creation he is an amalgam of several people.

'When Benignus was forming in my head my old teacher certainly was a huge element and there were other people I met through life who had some quality or other that came to bear. I think it gives truth to the characters we meet and feeds into what I do. There are also elements in Benignus that I like to think are part of me. There's a reflective side, maybe a kindness, and at the start of the book when he feels a little spider his other senses are developed as they've been sharply honed. The gentleness with which he deals with the spider on his hand and how he eases it down on to the rock is something that I admire in people.'

Ré is the author of more than twenty books. Many are multi-layered stories filled with a mix of barbarity and beauty, of good and evil coupled with intrigue. Imaginative leaps play a big part but a vital topographical aspect of the Burren that informs his writing is the place names.

'When I came to live here I abandoned my work every Tuesday and walked the hills, fields and limestone for many years. I got to know it well as a layman and took an interest in place names using Tim Robinson's Folding Landscapes map. I find it hard to look at a name and not wonder where it came from. It's not so much a passion as a quirkiness for me. If I can't figure it out I'll go and try to find the basis of the word so that I've a fairly educated notion as to where it comes from.

'In the Burren, names such as Ballyallaban, *Baile na hAille Báine*, mean the "townland of the white cliff". If you stand on the Ballyallaban ring fort near the Aillwee cave you will see the cliff of Aillwee which means "the yellow cliff" but there are times of the day when it is not yellow but white and I suspect that is why it was called *Baile na hAille Báine.'*

The idyllic place that he has made his home for two decades has helped his writing beyond measure. Through his long association with the Burren, there are several locations that are special to him. One of his favourites is right on his doorstep – Lough Rask, *Loch Reasca*, a mere 250m from his house and for him a place of magic.

'It is a tidal turlough which is rare and it is influenced not just by the water table but by water off the mountains but is also affected by the tide. At certain times, if you put your finger in, it is pure freshwater, at other times you get a saline element. Historically the story goes that on the eve of the battle of Corcomroe one of the O'Brien factions made camp at Lough Rask in 1317. On that night a fictitious supernatural figure called Dismal of the Burren – a hag of severe countenance – appeared to the soldiers and scared them. Many of them were bloodied and threw themselves in the lake. She had a horrific portent that very few would walk from the field at the battle. Whether she appeared or not – and I'm open on it – or whether it was a construct that came after the battle, I don't know. But it is an enchanting lake full of intrigue with a supernatural circle loved by walkers and bird watchers. A few years ago eighteen adult herons used to commute 300m from the lake to the sea and it was a great sight.'

There are other parts of the Burren that he loves. The megalithic tomb and quarry at *Páirc na Binne,* 'field of the peak', near Kilnaboy has resonance for him as well as the Gleninsheen box-tomb. 'There's something about the box-tomb's tidiness, about where it is and the remnants of the mound that I like.'

At any given time in his writing life, Ré can find himself working on two or three books. He toggles between writing in English and Irish and enjoys the thrill of working in both languages. 'The language is not a barrier – in fact I like to think it's an enhancer, whether it's contemporary or traditional in style. I wrote both *Terror on the Burren* and *Battle for the Burren* in English originally but the Irish language versions were first published. When I translate them I don't bother to look at the original. I just work from my head but they end up being identical except that idiomatically of course languages are different and the idioms of Irish for me are enhancers in my English work.

'At my talks I always tell the kids that I write two books at one time – look, you've got two hands so why leave one of them idle? They certainly don't get in the way of one another. If anything, they're complementary. I love working in English with the clear cut clinicalism of it as a language. Irish is the opposite as it is hugely poetic and takes the mind to places you couldn't dream.

'For me the Irish language is a passion and when you see how Hiberno-English is revered, I always think it's such a bastard form as it can only be some diluted form of both those languages. Irish lends itself to the place names of the Burren, the musicality and everything about the Burren which in its establishment was back in the time of Irish being spoken here. If you listen carefully to the speech of this area, what you get is *Béarla i gclúmh na Gaeilge,* 'English in the plumage of Irish'. People here speak English in beautiful reverse forms. For example, I have often heard them say: "Is it the way that . . ." *An amhlaidh go bhfuil . . .* which in terms of sequencing of words are forms directly from Irish. It would be a pity if they disappeared but when they're gone there's a huge loss. Unfortunately Irish got tied up and identified with the political movement which was a great pity where language is concerned.'

Clearly the Burren, and its associated topography, history, linguistic and cultural heritage, has offered Ré a deep well of inspiration as it has so many writers, painters and musicians. He does not consider himself an expert on it but believes the stimulation it provides is endless because people are diverse.

'We engage and encounter it in different ways as we all have a perspective on things. What fills the heart of one person won't be what fills the heart of another. Artists are instruments and we have something that necessitates and demands release so it's how we interpret it, how we take it in and what goes on in the subconscious that feeds into it. I feel you must be open to it but I'm not so sure you can consciously make yourself open to the Burren. It is a constant well and that is why you get repeated generations of people coming to it, whether it's Westropp or Praeger, Heaney or Longley.'

There are many demands on Ré's time. He has been busy promoting his latest novel, *Osama, Obama, Ó a Mhama!* for the 10–12 age group, that he describes as a quirky rollercoaster of an adventure. After my visit he is booked for interviews with Radio Kerry about the translation text he has done for Ann Marie McCarthy's children's book on Fungie the Dingle dolphin. Slots are lined up later in the day on Raidió na Gaeltachta and Clare FM.

Ré is never short of words in interviews but he rises to the challenge of being asked to sum up the Burren in one word. He glances out through the window of *An Scríobhlann* where the shadow of the midday sun moves slowly across the white icing-like limestone of Móinín Mountain, and replies monosyllabically 'Mesmeric,' then as an afterthought adds 'It engages the soul, the heart, the mind.'

Author Ré Ó Laighléis at his home at Lough Rask © Trevor Ferris

14

The Tinker's Heartbreak: Burren Roads

What is this life if, full of care,
We have no time to stand and stare.

W. H. Davies, 'Leisure'

'The older people always knew it,' a man once told me, 'as The Tinker's Heartbreak.' It is a stretch of road that runs long and straight, without so much as a kink for several kilometres. In the days when the tinkers walked the roads of Ireland they thought some would never end and that they might never reach their destination.

From the Corker Pass to the Khyber Pass, over Corkscrew Hill and around the great longueur sweeps of Ballyallaban Hill, the Burren is rich in crooked, mountainy roads. One of the best-known, with winding gradients, is the road between Ballyvaughan and Lisdoonvarna called Corkscrew Hill. A stopping place for tour coaches, it allows visitors to drink in outstanding views from the top. An old black and white photograph reproduced in books shows that the road, as well as the view, has been untouched by time and by the European Union's roadbuilding funds; it has changed little in a hundred years.

The most-loved Burren road (for visitors at least) is undoubtedly the coastal route, the R477, that runs 29km from Ballyvaughan to Doolin. It is a dramatic and scenic road for appreciation of the hills, flora, seascapes and views over Galway Bay. In summer it is packed with coaches, minibuses, parties of cyclists oozing lycra, power walkers, joggers and snoggers, but the best time to drive it is the spring – preferably on a bright evening to catch the light and watch dusk settle over the bay. Few forty-minute drives anywhere in Europe offer such a spectacular road so close to the sea for a large part of the journey.

I have spent many days vagabondising these byways and back roads, stopping to look, noticing things that take my fancy and moseying around. The Tinker's Heartbreak, marked on maps as the New Line, runs single track for 16km in a graceful arc along the eastern periphery of the Burren from Corcomroe towards Gort.

Once you cross out of it, heading inland, you have left behind the Burren and said farewell to its walls, terracing and pavement. Along its different stretches the road offers a magical sense of what the Burren is, providing an overview looking into it. Its hills compete for your attention as you gaze up at them, into its valleys and across its flatlands. Early one June morning I once walked most of its length and for the first half-hour I met no cars and no people along its narrow width. There were no comings or goings on the road. Not a farmer, shepherd, milkman or even milkmaid – not a travelling man, woman, child, or tinker bade me the time of day.

Like so many parts of the Burren, the road's evocative place names tell their own story: Corranroo, Shanclogh, Funshin More and Funshin Beg; Gortnaclogh, Cappah More, Tulla and Cushacorra. Its hedges are brimful and high. It is a road that speaks of an older land, one that possesses a strangeness, a road that for many may have represented a *via dolorosa*.

Another road well-known to me, having cycled, walked and driven it scores of times, is the R480, denoted by a thick, red line on the Ordnance Survey map and classified as a regional road. It runs past the cottage where I stay linking Ballyvaughan with the southern Burren and opening the door to Sheshymore, Mullaghmore, Leamaneh and Kilfenora. The Ballyallaban road gently twists and turns south of Aillwee cave and is one of *the* great mountain roads, not only of the Burren and Clare, but of all Ireland. It is not particularly steep although the views from it are spectacular. It has flowing corners as well as left and right hairpin bends. All this means that it has earned its place as a special road for the annual hill climb organised by Galway Motor Club.

One year, my visit coincided with the event and although it is not in my top 1,000 interests, I went along as a non-specialist spectator, whose history of owning 'exotic' road racing motor cars includes a Morris Minor, Mini, Renault 5, and Nissan Bluebird – all driven into the ground or round the clock several times. The climb attracts more than eighty drivers and motor sport enthusiasts from all over the country. Each year, on the last Sunday in April, they come in their Porsches, Minis, souped-up Hillman Imps and Ford Anglias. Sponsored by engineering works, garages, guttering firms, banks, bars, hotels, restaurants and plant hire companies, they gather on Sunday morning to break Ballyallaban bread and discuss road and weather conditions as well as the general state of motoring.

Starting on the main road near the cave entrance, the climb runs just over 3km to Lisgoogan. When I arrive dozens of drivers and mechanics are tuning up, revving engines, inflating tyres, checking screws and tightening exhausts. Yellow-coated, baseball-capped marshals direct traffic into fields that have become car parks for the day. They turn away visiting day-trippers and tourists who have accidentally stumbled upon Ireland's longest and fastest hill climb.

Rally drivers who tackle all the hill climbs throughout the country call Ballyallaban 'the big one'. One of the drivers, a fresh-faced sixty-something whose name tag on his navy boiler suit says Dennis, exchanges pleasantries from the comfort of his single-seater yellow Avenger. He has been coming for each of the past forty years of the sprint championship.

'Never missed a year since it started in the 1960s,' he says. 'We all love this hill. I call it bravery hill because it takes courage to drive up it at high speed.'

Dennis describes himself as a 'gentleman racer' rather than a 'boy racer'. He explains what is so special about the climb. 'The corner flows on it are slightly banked in some places and the road generates a great rhythm on a quick run. I would describe it as being like a smooth, continuous snake. It has a longitudinal groove which, when you take it right, is very satisfying. It commands great respect and rewards skilful driving.'

The hill climb is run over a demanding section of road presenting a unique challenge. At any one time during the climb there are six cars on it either racing up or returning to the starting blocks at a more sedate pace.

'They are very tight on the noise regulations compared to years ago,' says Dennis. 'Nowadays we all have silencers and we must be socially responsible although I've often compared the noise to a helicopter flying through your living room. There's a great thrill in it and a tremendous feeling of accomplishment when you've done it. We put total trust in the marshals to make sure the roads are clear of any people straying on to them.'

The Tinker's Heartbreak

I wish Dennis luck and walk over to watch the blood-red flag being lowered. A double white line across the road and a temporary set of traffic lights (the only ones ever in use in the Burren) marks the start line. As they wait patiently for the green light, the first cars are puttering. Like Scalextric racing toys they zoom off, shimmering and swaying, bouncing along the straight 100-metre opening stretch through a road tunnel overhung with a tangle of bright green trees and flying past hedges and roadsides sprinkled with clumps of dandelion, herb Robert, and the delicate blue germander speedwell which helps speed these travellers on their way.

An orange Riley Elf emits a sharp shotgun-like blast startling spectators and causing a frisson of excitement. The smell – much-loved by rally car enthusiasts – of burning rubber and fumes envelops the air. And despite the silencers they still manage to generate a substantial amount of noise. I climb over a wall and walk through fields to see if I can pick up the cars farther along the road. People stand behind walls chatting and laughing. Others gather beside Ballyallaban ring fort sited on a corner near the start. This was a religious and political nerve-centre and one of the most important settlements in the Burren although its history is today of no consequence to those standing around its doughnut-shaped base topped with tall trees.

At the first sweeping corner the scenery opens up showing off hills and valleys and I gaze down into the hazy and sunny green valley of Gragan East and across to the zigzag Corkscrew Hill. Each side of the road is lined with low walls and scrub. Early purple orchids, daisies, primroses and early flowering mountain avens line the verges, some of which are being cut up by the cars. At certain times, in the brief interregnum between races, spectators are permitted to walk quickly across the road. Some bravados follow its continuous central white line before jumping nimbly on to the limestone when the motorbike marshals with orange flashing lights appear round a corner with their 'get-outta-my-way' alarm signals.

Farther along, at Cahermore, an opening beside a farm gate allows spectators to look down on the drivers rattling through the gears coming out of a hairpin spitting loose stones. Behind them, unseen and uninspected, lies Cahermore stone fort built in the early medieval period as a defended farmstead of a wealthy Burren landowner. It has two walls – a strong inner wall enclosing a circular area and a lintelled gateway with small rooms built into its side walls. A sign informs me that the gateway is not original and may have been built in the fifteenth century to replace a simpler entrance. The outer stone-walled enclosure was sub-divided by thin walls which may have held animals. Archaeology, mixed with motor sport, may seem a strange combination but I find it a racy cocktail.

Time to move on; red-flagged marshals usher the crowd back or shoo them smartly along to the next viewing point. It reminds me of a different version of the annual spectator sport of bull-running in Pamplona. Some of those here are looking frantically for a gap in a hedge or trying to high-jump a wall in a desperate scramble for safety. Hell hath no fury like a Ballyallaban Hill climber – whose every millisecond is a matter of life or death – trying to dodge a stray wanderer.

I take my life in my hands and walk quickly over to the other side before climbing higher on to the limestone terracing to look down the road at the cars and across to the wide northern section of the Burren. From this vantage point near Gleninsheen there is no human habitation – not a house in sight, not a chimney smoking, just cars at full throttle smoking their way to the top.

At Lisgoogan a white painted line with the letter 'F' marks the end. Here the road plateaus out before plunging downhill towards Poulnabrone. The finish line denotes the spot tucked away behind a gate in a field where, according to a sign, Paddy

Nolan discovered the 'very precious collar of gold in 1932'. The Gleninsheen collar found here is now on display in the National Museum in Dublin. A yellow Bronze Age gold collar, a replica of the shape of the original one and dated 700BC, has been carved into the stone and erected by his friends.

Ballyallaban Hill is a road rich in antiquity and full of quirky diversions that have become familiar waymarks to me. The surrounding area from Aillwee and Ballycahill, through Berneens to Gleninsheen and Lisgoogan drips with a rich past and is polished with history. Apart from some of the treasures already mentioned, you will also find adjacent to the roadside, holy wells (one for an eye cure and the other a toothache cure), megalithic tombs, several crosses and cists. In the townland of Ballyallaban near the starting line sits a bullaun stone beside a circular area of raised ground with a late cross standing on an altar-like platform. It is believed there was an early monastic settlement here but it has not been recorded.

Once a year, the road is crowded with the snarl of high-octane engines, smells and fumes producing a decibel level which, although now strictly controlled, is nonetheless uncharacteristic of the Burren. For a few hours, the peace of this area is destroyed. Birdsong is drowned, wind noise is barely noticeable, the normally still atmosphere evaporates in a cloud of smoke while bemused cattle and sheep are unsure what has happened to their world of serenity. Not a hare or stoat is to be seen, the butterflies have disappeared into a late diapause and the feral goats have wandered off elsewhere in search of tranquillity. Car sirens clear the roads and for one afternoon the hill represents 3.5 fun-loving, hair-raising, thrill-seeking kilometres of tarmac producing an adrenalin rush for drivers and spectators.

This Burren road, normally full of coaches, minibuses and camper vans as well as cyclists and walkers, gives pleasure for one day to several hundred people for a completely different reason.

Burren Country

Like so many of the Burren's storied roads, this one has much to tell. On this day it shares its twists and bends, its archaeological, cultural and floristic heritage, with some of Ireland's fastest mountain men on four wheels indulging in what can only be regarded as extreme noise terror.

Corkscrew Hill © Trevor Ferris

15
Bard of Bell Harbour

How can I lie in a lukewarm bed
With all the thoughts that come into my head?

Brian Merriman, *The Midnight Court*

The shhh! police are on duty as the bearded musician launches into a gravelly version of 'Sweet Ballyvaughan'. Quickly the talk dies and the raw singing voice takes over, stunning the audience into silence.

It is a wet Monday night at the end of August and the rain hammers against the windows. Inside in the warmth more than forty people, tourists and locals, are squeezed into Greene's bar. Small knots of English, Dutch, Norwegians and Germans as well as a scattering of Americans sit at tables with pints or wine glasses anticipating the next song and watching with admiration.

A work-related conversation by two women at a table is hushed by those deeming it sacrilege to talk across a musical session. Whispered words are exchanged by two Dutchmen between songs but they break off mid-sentence as the musician erupts into full voice. They have come to hear one of the supreme singers not just of the Burren, Clare or the west of Ireland, but of the whole country.

Seán Tyrrell is the Real McCoy, not a folksy imitation or a one-man stage-Irish performance to please the tourists; he is a singer with a unique style, crafted and honed over four decades of poetic music-making. He has a remarkable power to distract his audience from their daily worries and transport them to foreign lands. Ballads and traditional songs flow as fast as the pulling of the pints. With consummate ease and without preamble Seán moves from soft songs of love, loss and desire to impassioned five-minute cameos about vagabonds, wanderers and gypsies alongside tales of exile, longing, separation, heartbreak and death all wrapped up in a swell of melancholic emotion.

An appreciative response greets the instrumental 'Midnight in the Burren' while 'Game Over' starts with an engaging declarative opening: 'See the blood spout, steaming, gleaming. Dark the ocean . . .' The tempo is slowed down with the lyrical 'One Starry Night' followed by a brisk version of 'All the Wild Young Children'.

Much to the chagrin of customers, an American woman sitting with two others punches numbers on her mobile phone and before placing it on the table insists to her friend in California – you *must* listen to this:

> I'm just lying here dreaming about you now,
> Wondering if you have found your way from last year
> Your topsy-turvy friends have left you in an empty shell.

A seasoned practitioner in the art of crowd-pleasing both at home and on the other side of the world, Seán switches with relaxed versatility from tenor guitar to banjo and a repertoire of songs, new and old, interspersed with jigs and reels. For twenty-five years he has been a summer fixture in a corner of Greene's on

Monday and Wednesday nights. In-the-know locals are joined by visitors, some of whom have stumbled in by happenstance or have seen a small sign on the window advertising 'Live Traditional Music Tonight: 9.30 p.m.'

Many have no idea of the stature of this unpretentious musical wizard performing before them contentedly, informally and almost casually but with heartfelt sensitivity. They may not be aware that he has produced five CDs and two DVDs, and is renowned and respected throughout the international world of Irish music. 'Amazing voice,' a Dublin man standing at the bar mutters to no one in particular. 'I drove here especially to hear him singing and to see how he can command a pub.'

One of Seán's strengths is reinventing songs, switching from the exuberant to the intense sometimes with a forceful urgency that can shake tourists out of their holiday lethargy. Old and, in some cases, forgotten classics, such as 'Side by Side', 'Time You Old Gypsy Man' and 'John O' Dreams' may be rooted in the past but tonight he brings them alive reincarnating them with a new dynamism. The foot- and finger-tappers, hand-clappers and singalong swayers join in 'South of the Border (Down Mexico Way') before musical journeys to Kathmandu and the Yukon.

But mostly, the searing voice, pure in tone and immeasurably beautiful, reflects the spirit of the local environment: the limestone rocks and stones, the sea, the dancing orchids and gentians, and the wildness of his adopted part of north Clare. The chatter is increasing again but just a few bars into 'The Lights of Christmas' – a poignant Burren tale of emigration, hope and love – the small room falls completely silent.

During a break Seán talks across the tables to a New Yorker about life in the city where he used to live. They enjoy a joke about the Irish summer rain. He orders a drink and from his seat surveys the bar for a few minutes before a short instrumental leads into the anti-war song 'The 12th of July' followed by 'The

Faltering Flame', a song about the peace process in Northern Ireland. After three hours of sustained, high quality solo musicianship, a mellow and satisfied feeling runs through the crowd as the wall lights flash on and off signifying last orders. Six customers at the counter wave notes at the barmaid working flat out to cope with final thirst demands. Talking stops, orders are mouthed quietly and a hush returns as the distinctive voice resonates across the crowded room bouncing off the walls with the opening lyrics from 'The Coast of Malabar': 'Far awaaaaay across the ocean beneath an Indian star . . .'

A sense of intimacy pervades and those present realise they are privileged to have spent an evening in the company of one of *the* great contemporary musical talents. Heads full of images conjured through the mellifluous music, they drain their glasses and pull on their anoraks, nodding acknowledgement to the figure gathering up his musical instruments, before disappearing into the dark wet Burren night. They have found that frequently elusive *craic* – not the clichéd *craic* beloved of tourist board copywriters – and will return home content that Ireland can still produce special nights of magic. And in their minds the lyrics from songs such as 'John O' Dreams' echo as a takeaway memory: 'Midnight has come and the good people homeward thread'.

Perhaps one day, heeding the admonition contained in Seán's exquisitely haunting 'Sweet Ballyvaughan' ' . . . they'll return cross the sea, to the Burren, to me and to Clare'.

～～～

To find out more about his musical influences, Seán invited me to come the next day and talk to him at his house in Dooneen near Bell Harbour. His stone cottage, which is set in a hollow, looks out on to a narrow stretch of water called *Poll Dubhda*, 'the Black Hole'.

Bard of Bell Harbour

He was born in Galway in 1943 into a musical family and his playing days stretch back to the 1960s when he performed in the Folk Castle club in the city. In 1968 he emigrated to America and played professionally singing in Irish bars in New York and San Francisco on what he calls 'the-corned-beef-and-cabbage circuit'. He returned home in 1976 and went to live in Kerry before deciding to move to Clare where he was appointed caretaker at University College Galway's research station at Carron. One day he was walking with a friend at Eagle's Rock in the heart of the Burren when something about the place spoke to him.

'It was only then that I began to realise what the Burren was all about. I was ignorant of its importance and the significance of it prior to that as I never came here as a child. I remember a tangible feeling came over me and I said to myself, "I have finally found my spiritual homeland." I went up Slievenaglasha, which has many legends attached to it and had an overwhelming feeling that this is the place where our ancestors retreated to. There is fertile land up there and it had a huge effect on me. It's hard to quantify the reason but something touched me about it. When I lived in the States I had at least four or five different homes but I knew that this was the place, and especially here in Bell Harbour, where I wanted to live.

'One of the most immediate things I loved about it was the people. The neighbours are generous and helpful. If I need a job done farmers will bring their tractors to help out and they'll bring you topsoil if you need it. There's a lovely spirit about this place and I've been welcomed with open arms.'

Seán looks back on how his poetic-musical life took off. One night he was asked to play in a pub in Lisdoonvarna. 'The barman said he wanted some songs so I was flicking through a book of poems and 'Bagpipe Music' by Louis MacNeice caught my imagination. I found it hilarious and knew immediately this was the song for me. I sat down and quickly produced some incredible stuff – and unquestionably being in the Burren influenced that. I started to sing poems and realised this was what I was looking for. I didn't want to do "The Wild Rover" or "Black Velvet Band" – they've been done to death by some groups and have become an abomination but I wanted to find other things and that's where the poetry book came in useful.'

That book was one that Seán found in New York called *1000 Years of Irish Poetry*. It remained with him through his travels, and for many years has provided creative nourishment and sustenance. One of the poets that most intrigued him was John Boyle O'Reilly who was born in County Louth in 1844. In a CD in 2009, *Message of Peace*, he recounts the story of O'Reilly's life in song and words. Beginning with dialogue, the double album includes songs invoking the poetry of Francis Ledwidge, Charles Lever, Oscar Wilde, John Lennon and Bobby Sands.

'When I read O'Reilly's first poem I was flabbergasted by it and couldn't believe the style in which it was written,' Seán says. 'It was ideal material for songs so I set them to music and it is the trilogy on my first solo album *Cry of the Dreamer* released in 1994. He joined the Fenian movement and then the English cavalry hoping to infiltrate key regiments and instigate a general rebellion until they were sold out by an Irish informer.'

O'Reilly was sentenced to death which was later commuted to life imprisonment, and was sent on a convict ship to Fremantle in Australia. He escaped on a whaling ship to America. Later he became editor of the *Boston Pilot*, a leading Irish-American newspaper and went on to rise to a position of influence in US politics and literature. His poems on Irish and American themes mostly deal with the heroism of the common soldier.

'His life is such a gripping story,' Seán says. 'He was a true internationalist making common cause with the American

Indian and the African-American at a time when both peoples were denied the most basic rights.'

The Burren gave Seán the chance to develop a connection between poetry and music which is his passion. The range of poetic voices that he has tapped into stretches from the eighteenth century Clare poet Brian Merriman and C. D. Shanley, through Yeats, MacNeice and Kavanagh up to Seamus Heaney and Paul Durcan. This standing army also includes Michael Hartnett, Mary O'Malley and Rita Ann Higgins.

Living in the Burren has been inspiring for Seán as he is surrounded by music and many renowned musicians. 'Chris Droney, the great concertina player, lives near me, as well as Mike Fahy, Micko Russell and Tommy Peoples. Davy Spillane would often join our sessions so it couldn't help but influence me and the atmosphere of the Burren began to affect me in ways I didn't even realise and definitely coloured the music that came out of me.

'I'm labelled a songwriter but I'm not really a songwriter as I've only written three full songs in my life. I always thought I would have the gift for words and not for music but was surprised when I found it was the reverse. And I was delighted that I had the gift of composition. I'm more of a thief of other people's ideas. I describe myself as a reporter delivering and reporting what these poets and writers said.'

Like so many creative artists who live in the area, Seán has experienced numerous special moments. 'Everything comes into the Burren equation with me. In the days when I was oyster farming I would be up to my belly in water with a wetsuit and I remember that a swan used to come and visit me at Muckinish. It would stand and look at me, then wander off again, and return and do it again. The sea bed is fascinating and the different colours of seaweeds never cease to amaze me. One summer's day I was coming in by boat and noticed the whole sea floor covered in incredibly beautiful white lace which was like a sea mushroom. I had never seen anything like it.

'Along this boreen where I live when you reach the sea at Bell Harbour there's a bed of the most magnificent mussels. There is something special about picking them and carrying them up to the house. I used to sell mussels for years and supplied them to some of the best restaurants along the west coast. It was extremely hard work but I still like going there. The very smell of my hands when I come back is like perfume to me even though it is muck and dirt but I just love eating them with friends after I've picked them fresh. I enjoy walking along different parts of the shore and discovering places where you find seaweeds, razorfish, cockles, oysters, or different types of scallop. The oysters from here are famous – in fact Henry VIII used to demand his oysters came from *Poll Dubhda*.'

Seán has been working on a new show in Irish and English called 'Who Killed James Joyce?' Again this weaves together the muse and music tapping into a rich poetic spectrum.

'In a BBC interview that I came across, MacNeice read his poem "Prognosis" and I've included it in the show. It was written in Galway in 1939 and he said it was like a children's rhyme but with foreboding. When he read it I recognised the internal rhythm and tune. I'm also using a Heaney poem simply called "Poem", and a Mary O'Malley poem "Hormones". I discovered the best way of doing it is to break down the individual parts of the poem. Some such as "Bagpipe Music" fall readily as it is like a variation of the tune of "Pop Goes the Weasel".'

Seán's admirers have their own favourite songs. 'The Coast of Malabar', which is a waltz, is one of his most requested. 'That would have been a regular one I heard when I was growing up along with Robert Service's "The Cremation of Sam McGee" which my uncle Paddy used to recite. Another often requested song is "Sweet Ballyvaughan", the tune for which was written by a Glasgow woman Judi McKeown who lived here, fell in love and got broken-hearted.'

One of the biggest projects of Seán's musical career involved tackling Merriman's *The Midnight Court*. He became fascinated with the bawdy epic poem written in 1780 which is regarded as one of the most important and comic contributions to Gaelic literature. 'I was working in a hostel in Kerry and a hosteller left a copy of David Marcus' translation of it. I began to read it and was floored with laughter. Other writers had translated it but I thought his version was beautiful and decided to put some of it to music. Then I thought I would do the whole thing and took sections of it and worked on it over a winter. I wrote out the title of the tunes and sang the whole lot into a tape recorder. It had to be ballsy and gutsy and when we performed it in Galway it had a great reaction and was a big hit everywhere we went with it.

'So again I was just the reporter. Merriman wrote the poem, Marcus translated it and he didn't make an attempt to write a poem in English to equal the original in flowery language. But he got the humour across and doesn't pull any punches.'

Through his linking of music and poetry Seán has built up an unrivalled collection of songs but curiously for a professional musician he does not like listening to himself singing. 'I constantly say "Thanks-be-to-God I don't like the sound of my own voice." If someone comes here and wants to hear something on CD I have to leave the room. I do listen to the songs in the car to critique them but that doesn't happen very often. What I feel I can do best is deliver a great lyric. That's the first, last and most important thing to me, and to do it clearly. My antenna is always tuned. I'm always looking and searching and I hope it never stops.'

Apart from the banjo, which is his first love, and tenor guitar, Seán specialises in playing instruments from the same family: the mandolin, the mandolo, the mandocello and the mandobass.

'For the commercial fellas I'm not commercial enough and for the folk people I'm not folksy enough. Sometimes it works against me but there's nothing I can do about it and people find it hard to pigeon-hole me. I really don't care. I often ask people to tell me any one song about emigration that is supposedly within the canon of Irish traditional music that has lines such as "Galway Bay": 'For the strangers came and tried to teach us their ways, They scorned us just for bein' what we are, But they might as well go chasin' rainbows . . .' Just because Bing Crosby sang it does not make it a bad song.'

Aficionados of the genre reckon Seán Tyrrell is one of the best, and have known this for a long time. In the early 1990s he was described by fellow Clare musician P. J. Curtis as 'simply the most intensely moving, soulful and talented singer of ballads and traditional songs in Ireland'. In the intervening twenty years he has maintained that position and enhanced his reputation with his recordings and live performances. Curtis writes of 'a strange current of electricity which passes from his heart and soul directly to his audience'.

The sleeve notes on Seán's *Belladonna* CD with its atmospheric photograph taken inside Ó Loclainn's bar in Ballyvaughan, comes with a mental health warning: 'I have been accused of being a Romantic, melancholic and sometime cynic. This CD is liberally laced with the first two and touches of the latter.' Seán elaborates on this, explaining what gives him most satisfaction in his performances. 'What I try to do in my singing is not to get people to say that they loved the lyrics. The most important thing for me is that people leave saying what an incredible song that was. If they don't, then I haven't done my job properly. If there's a message in it then I have done my job well. There was a famous session which used to be held on Sunday afternoons in the Róisín Dubh pub in Galway and it was always a packed house. Someone once said to me later that he had been drawn to tears by a song called "The Orchard" and I thought I must be doing something right as I drew emotion.

'I want to leave the audience with something that is worthwhile. I don't have many accolades but it's tremendous to think that I might have touched people in some way at the end of the night and that they've gone away with food for thought. Now that's worth something.'

Musician Seán Tyrrell at his home in Bell Harbour © Trevor Ferris

16

The Weavers of Sheshymore

No ground or floor
is as kind to the human step
as the rain-cut flags
of these white hills.

Porous as skin,
limestone resounds sea-deep, time-deep,
yet, in places, rainwater has worn it thin
as a fish's fin.

Moya Cannon, 'Thirst in the Burren'

Few manage to make their way into it, but those who do take the trouble, find themselves in an area with an unbounded sense of freedom, a veritable limestone landscape de luxe, and a place where you could be forgiven for thinking that the earth is cracking open. Sheshymore is hard to locate and does not flaunt itself. It is not visible from the roadside because it is hidden by an impenetrable tangle of tall, thick clumps of hazel trees interwoven with sharp, thorny bushes, brambles, nettles and thistles concealing grykes and forming a barrier to deter all but the most determined.

Its inaccessibility means that it is a peaceful few acres of limestone. Not many choose to pause here and prise their way through the undergrowth. Even though I have been to it more than a dozen times, I still have trouble gaining an entry and have been frustrated trying to find a way in. On several occasions I have given up since I had not enough time to work out how to access it. On another occasion I plunged my foot and leg into a gryke covered with grassy tussocks, drawing blood and leaving a legacy of an 8cm-long bruise that changed from red to blue and then deep purple. The bruise stayed with me for several weeks reminding me of the suffering that is sometimes made for art, or at least in finding an uncelebrated section of limestone pavement.

So where exactly is it? If you were to draw two lines forming a large X over a Burren map, Sheshymore would lie some way south of the intersection of those lines tucked away amongst the Burren's cartographic nooks and crannies although it is not a place to take your grannies. From a topographic point of view it is best located through the better known place names surrounding it: north of Leamaneh, south of Carron church, west of Mullaghmore and east of Ballyganner.

Peaceably, it lies undisturbed in the south central section of the Burren. It is 24km inland so does not attract the seaside trippers, sightseers or tourists in search of big waves. The mountain avens growing here, sheltered from the sea, wind and rain, look much healthier than those along the coast at Black Head.

Sheshymore straddles the main Ballyvaughan to Kilnaboy road although most of it is concentrated on the western side of this road. The best way into it is to leave the main road at the T-junction from Carron, clamber through a breach in the wall and search for a way through the thick, mixed woodland. Walking sticks are recommended, not so much for support, but as beaters to help force a way through the tangle of dense vegetation. Masses of silverweed, with its distinctive gleamy silver foliage (which does not seem to mind being trampled) along with meadowsweet, cuckoo-spit and willowherb, grows comfortably alongside circular cow pats.

I had read in Westropp's *Archaeology of the Burren* a reference to the Sheshy forts, Cahermore and Caheraclarig. I liked their euphony and one day in need of an excuse to cross Sheshymore, I thought I would try to locate them. On the Folding Landscapes map they are shown close together and are the two forts nearest the road. In Irish they appear as *Cathair Mhor* and *Cathair an Chiáraigh.* Megalithic tombs, cists, souterrains and cairns lie all around on the edge of the townland. Within a 5km radius, I count no fewer than twenty-seven archaeological monuments dotted across the map. After clambering up a small grass and stony bank I reach the limestone within a few minutes. Once found Sheshymore is worth taking time to explore. At first glance there is not much to see but it is a microcosm of the wider Burren. An extensive open expanse of limestone, it contains one of the longest and most complete sections to be found anywhere.

This vast but little-known oasis is characterised by long slabs of continuous and unbroken crisscrossed pavement, undamaged and with a clean metallic sheen. So far inland, the sea has not washed it and few if any tourists tramp its huge, rectangular, table-like clints that look so flat they might have been ironed to a pristine smoothness. Wide grykes stretch north–south in straight deep cuts for hundreds of metres or as far as the eye can see.

On the colourful geological map of the Burren, Sheshymore is given the classification 'be' standing for Ballyelly Member and is shaded light grey similar to the colour of the pavement. The specific brand of bedrock found here is described as 'nodular and with chert'. Chert is a flint-like form of quartz composed of chalcedony. There are aspects of the outdoor appearance of the place that make it stand out as being different from other areas. The most obvious signs are the absence of stone walls and the lack of grassland in its central core. Although trees surround the area, they are not found in large numbers on the limestone and apart from the occasional erratic, nothing interrupts the long horizon.

Wordsworth would have loved it. He always wrote walking up and down or in a spot where the continuity of his verse would not be interrupted although he would have had to have been careful of the grykes and may not have approved of the lack of daffodils. The views stretch several kilometres to all points of the compass. To the east the ground rises slightly, but mostly it is a flat, plateau-like landscape. I try to work out the best route to explore it to find Westropp's forts. Although I am on a quest, the idea of a wander at will appeals to me. A plane streaks overhead and I glance up. The clouds sit low here but the sky is vast, a mirror of this wide open area. Put someone in the picture and they are insignificant in this place. Two photographers who have accompanied me on visits have both stared open-mouthed across the landscape before spreadeagling themselves on the limestone. On all my visits I have never come across anyone else. The creatures of the natural world know about it and are well represented. Butterflies, bumblebees and hares are found trafficking here. They do not appear to have any difficulty locating its natural riches. At first sight there does not seem much to photograph with little evidence of the imprint of human activity yet photographers who have discovered the place have produced extraordinary images.

If you were to look down on this stretch of pavement with a robin's eye view, it is a complex mosaic of limestone reminiscent of the patterns on an Aran jumper – a spaghetti junction with a confluence of grykes and somewhere that at first glance could be mistaken for having experienced an earthquake. After brushing off bits of twigs and branches stuck to my T-shirt, trousers, socks and trainers, I set off from my entry point with birdsong my only company. Nonchalantly, a skylark advertises itself high up perhaps to attract a mate or to warn off intruders entering its territory. Coming from the surrounding trees and hedgetops, meadow pipits, wrens, and a yellowhammer – still looking for its *little-bit-of-bread-and-no-cheese* – all throw out their calls into the bright spring air.

The clints are firmly embedded without any of the usual wobbling associated with other areas. Bird's-foot trefoil and early purple orchids have a firm foothold. It is a warm May evening but the grykes with their miniature woodland habitat are damp and shady places. They are amongst the deepest I have come across. One stretches down for at least two metres. I plunge my metre-long blackthorn walking stick into its semi-darkness and discover that it does not even reach halfway to the bottom.

Honeysuckle, hart's-tongue fern and the pale greenish yellow flowers of wood sage flourish in the yawningly wide grykes. I also identify woodbine, plantain, the delicate wall lettuce with its small flowerheads and maroon stem, and the tiny green feathery spikes of lady's mantle. The crevices contain small patches of wall rue as well as holly and ivy, all typical woodland plants.

I stare at insignificant things that I find on the ground alongside the flowers: a solitary beehive with a delicate honeycomb; the fossil debris of crinoids and beside them hazel shells most likely opened by a wood mouse and with a remarkably clean incision. Strange are the things – Jim Perrin refers to 'the bright particularity of things' – that sidetrack you on a ramble.

Half-a-dozen tall clumps of hairy rock-cress with its

white flowers spring erectly from a gryke. Its name does not immediately conjure up a flower of singular beauty and as a member of the cabbage family, it is hardly one of the Burren's 'A' list of spectaculars, but I have always had a sneaking admiration for it and its exotic botanical name *Arabis hirsuta*. Searching around I come across more clumps of it – for me it is an exciting find and a previously undiscovered flower to tick off my list.

My dilly-dallying leads to an even more remarkable sight – spiders working busily in numerous grykes creating delicately woven orb webs. I peer into one and notice a large spider on overdrive. It is 7.00 p.m. and an early evening maintenance session is taking place. Kneeling on the ground for a micro look I consider how an eight-legged arachnid repairs the silk web of fibres strung across one of the grykes like a washing line. The gap measures about 4cm and the web is connected firmly to each side with long tightly woven straight diagonal web-lines. In the gryke it is well protected from the full force of buffeting wind. I flick my finger and feel the strength and elasticity – experts say they are many times stronger than steel and contain remarkable properties. In fact they are said to be the strongest natural fibre on earth.

For more than thirty minutes, under the shade of a small elderberry tree, I watch the spider at work. Painstakingly threading, nimbly running up and down, thrashing around industriously repairing the silk, it crisscrosses the concentric web with an all-consuming zeal. The intricate pattern of circles containing tiny rectangular box-like shapes of many different sizes (reminiscent of a map of America showing the individual states) is a remarkable feat of creative design. Sometimes the spider pauses, dangles for a short while, puzzling its next move, then turns around in circles again scurrying hither and thither, unconcerned at an intrusive spectator encroaching on its world. The spiders' webs here are similar to thousands found elsewhere but a scrutiny of a small weaver quietly going about its business in this special place is a memorable sight. Waylaid by Sheshymore's spiders and with darkness descending, I abandon my search for Westropp's forts and decide to leave them for another day – a perfect reason to return.

The Burren offers many dreamy places in which to linger and return to. But if you seek your own few private compressed hectares of limestone and somewhere with a profound sense of solitude, Sheshymore is *the* place to visit. A delectably secretive location, it retains a distinctive and largely unvisited character conferring a sense of ownership. Being here can feel like an intense trespass but it seems selfish not to share its lonely and elemental beauty with discerning readers and those who appreciate havens of ancient peace.

The Geological Society of Ireland has, without much fuss, designated Sheshymore as one of five sites in the Burren of international importance. Another seven are regarded by the geological community as being of national significance. If international awards were made for quiet, untrodden, epiphanic places then Sheshymore, laden with magic, and a sanctuary in which to escape from the madness of the world, would win the Nobel Peace Prize.

Uplifted after each visit and always with regret, I take my leave, buzzing with adrenaline and wishing I could remain for longer in this enclosed and exhilarating fold of the earth that soothes the troubled spirit. Being here induces a sense of inner peace. The top of Mullaghmore may be the place from which to shout your barbaric yawp but Sheshymore invokes the urge to cry out in ecstasy . . . especially after an hour considering the silky skills of a fine-spun web or even in pursuit of the hirsute.

Sheshymore pavement © Marty Johnston

Epilogue

Flirting with the Spirit of the Burren

It does not matter where his body lies for it is grass; but where his spirit is, it will be good to be.

Nicholas Black Elk, *Black Elk Speaks*

As I drove into Ballyvaughan one night as dusk was falling, a pine marten trotted swiftly across my path on the road at Ballyallaban before scampering over a stone wall. I caught my breath. It was an arresting moment and a defining experience, but within a few seconds our brief encounter was over. At first appearance I thought it was a cat. I had noted its luxuriant, thick, chocolate brown hair and creamy-yellow throat patch. Its local name is 'marten cat'. There was not time to swap glances but luckily I had a long enough glimpse of it, and its furry tail, to know that this was the seldom seen *Martes martes*. In fact

I have seen it only three times during my visits and in every case it was not a face-to-face encounter – more face-to-rapidly-disappearing tail, and mostly for a maximum of ten seconds. As one of Ireland's rarest native animals, it hides its light, mostly under bushes rather than bushels, partly owing to the fact that it is a nocturnal prowler with few daytime outings.

The pine marten likes well-developed ground vegetation. One of its favourite habitats is hazel scrub, and the Burren has an abundant supply of hazel trees for this agile climber. It thrives on the limestone and has adapted to spending time foraging on the open pavement. Pine marten love deserted cottages and derelict stone buildings where they can set up house in an undisturbed way; again the Burren has a plentiful offering of scattered, dilapidated buildings left by people who gave up trying to wring a living from this tough land. Their nests include hollow trees or holes in dry, rocky places – once more the Burren offers ideal territory. Their menu includes berries, fruits, and birds' eggs. They eat small insects, rabbits and birds and have been known to attack poultry. According to the naturalist James Fairley, they have 'extraordinary catholic tastes and a menu of greater diversity than any other Irish mammal'.

Given these considerations and the fact that the Burren has a pleasing absence of people, it is not surprising that this solitary night creature inclined to bashfulness and with feline features has a special love for the area and thrives here. It embodies its tutelary spirit. These are the reasons why this rarely seen night voyager survives.

I have often considered what has called me back to the Burren, why it exerts such an irresistible pull, and have tried to account for its centrality in my life. Like the pine marten, I am native to Ireland, enjoy fruit and although I have arboreal tendencies, I have no special longing to climb hazel trees, sniff bark, taste resin or live in derelict buildings. There has, though, always been a wandering streak to my life, complete with a bohemian vagrancy and a nocturnal side. I have tried to analyse my emotions and evolve my own disciplines as to why I have such a longing for the place and why I have spent a disproportionate amount of my life exploring its mysteries, banging my knees on its rock and occasionally falling into its grykes.

Since my late teens I have been fortunate to have travelled widely, visiting five continents and two hemispheres. My honeymoon was spent on a houseboat in Kashmir overlooking the Himalayas. I have driven the Great Ocean Road in Australia, toured New England in the fall, safaried in Kenya, tramped the jungles of Indonesia, ridden white horses through the Camargue, paid homage at the Taj Mahal and sunbathed in the Caribbean. I have wandered the streets of Florence, Venice, San Francisco, Istanbul, Marrakech, Prague, Seville, Barcelona, St Petersburg (when it was Leningrad), Paris, Amsterdam and many other cities.

The highest snowy hills of Scotland and Wales have called me to climb them. As a visiting Fellow, I have been enraptured by the honey-coloured buildings and colleges of Oxford (the view from the Radcliffe Camera has not changed in 500 years), and enjoyed the ceaseless life of London both for work and pleasure. Nearer home, I love the drumlins of my Tyrone childhood, the high peaks of Kerry and Connemara, the coastline of Donegal, the glens of Antrim and the rock art of County Meath's historic high places. Although I revel in the anonymity of cities, being a village boy at heart I love mooching around the streets of Ireland's small towns listening to the gossip and watching their twitching windows. I have spent time in many of them: from Kilmore Quay to Dunmore East, from Kenmare, Kinnitty and Cadamstown, through Oola and Oldcastle, Lismore and Ardmore; I have lingered in the North Tipperary duo of Coolbaun and Puckaun, have pondered in Pastimeknock (a townland in the Waterford

parish of Trinity Without), waited patiently for that Effin bus,
heard the dogs bark in Lattin, and misbehaved in the pubs of
Carrick-on-Shannon. Most of all, though, I have been happiest
whiling away the hours in Ballyvaughan.

We all have a collection of images of a place or places that
are of appeal. Each, in its own way, has at different times of
my life, been special. But when I think of where I *really* want
to be for supreme happiness, then it is pavement-pounding,
tramping the hills, breathing the crystalline air, and indulging in
the floristic pleasures of the grey limestone of the Burren. Like
the pine marten, I have my own reasons. It is a perpetual place,
a precious place, a dream place, and a dreamer's world. It is a
place that weaves an enduring spell with its sights and sounds,
its solaces and silences.

The ethereal beauty and sense of contentment found in it
has often called me back. It has been indispensable to my well-
being, cleansing the toxins and serving my spiritual needs. It
has become my uttermost desideratum. (Be still, my beating
heart!) The romantically inclined Welsh call it *hiraeth*: a longing
or yearning for the homeland or for something indefinable.
The Portuguese sum up this complexity of feelings in the word
saudade: an ache in one's soul, the feeling of missing something,
or homesickness. The Turks too have a word for this sadness:
huzun, which roughly translates as 'melancholy.' The American
nature writer Richard Nelson puts it well:

> What makes a place special is the way it buries itself inside
> the heart, not whether it's flat or rugged, rich or austere,
> wet or arid, gentle or harsh, warm or cold, wild or tame.
> Every place, like every person, is elevated by the love and
> respect shown toward it, and by the way in which its
> bounty is received.

When you are in it, the outside world can seem a thousand kilometres away. After each visit, having renewed my fix of Burren bounty in my happiness hotspots, all is right with the world. When Bill Bryson was crossing the remote, flat and empty lands of South Dakota in *The Lost Continent* he described it as 'the world's first drive-through sensory deprivation chamber'. He should have come to the Burren. Almost to the point of sensorial overload, my senses are in a state of heightened awareness, my horizons widened. With a revived eye I feel I can see farther and better appreciate images, shapes and colours. I leave in a happy mental and physical state, content that I can carry around in my head an archive of personal images. Like the paying of a good compliment, the golden afterglow of these images lasts for up to six months. Its physical finery and visual memory is forever in my mind's eye (partly owing to the fact that a framed Folding Landscapes map measuring 1.2m by 1m occupies a huge amount of wall space above my writing desk).

What then is the prevailing spirit of this stony, hill-swaddled place at the extreme edge of Europe, and how best can its intrinsic nature be captured? You will never capture the totality of it in words, photographs or paintings. You will find it hard to bottle the intoxicating nectar of the Burren for later consumption. (An entrepreneur once tried this in Cumbria and sold it in souvenir tins as Lake District Air.) The Burren nectar, which is something of an acquired taste, is extremely difficult to pin down. It is an elusive abstraction. Its essential spirit – the *sui generis* – will always remain intangible. The Burren holds many secrets. Interpreting its innermost inscrutable thoughts is not an easy challenge. People set out to capture it; instead it captures them. Richard Mabey describes it as a place of 'incongruity and optical illusion . . . an exuberant, flirtatious landscape'. There is no doubt you could spend a lifetime flirting with the smooth limestone and not do justice to its unending mystery. Yet its essence is to be found everywhere. Catch the right day and you can feel it in the ruins of an abbey or in a walk along a green road. You can sense it in the frolic of a butterfly, the swerve of a raven, the quiver of the wind-blown mountain avens, the pungent smell of wild garlic or the straw stalactites dangling in a cave with their mesmerising silver threads of light. You can sense it in the exhilaration of the wild waves on a clint at Poll Salach, during sunset at Black Head, a walk alongside the stream at Rathborney, in the curve of a mountain, the feel of the wind coming off the Atlantic, the shape of a stark erratic, the undulating and swift flight of a redpoll, or an hour spent seawatching. You can sense it in a night of beauty with a harvest moon of silver quietness and an element of melancholy hanging in the air.

The Burren possesses what are regarded as the five essential components for finding tranquillity in modern life: natural landscape, listening to birdsong, peace and quiet (a magnificent 'sound'), seeing natural-looking woodland, and a clear view of the stars. The daily snapshots and minute dramas – referred to by nature writers as 'encounters of meaning' – live long with those who visit. Incandescent visions of things I have seen often flit across my dreams. Occasionally it is the commonplace that stirs these super-charged memories, the accumulation of intense moments. The list, with details that are burned on my retina, includes vignettes from a day-long walk in the hills, a chance meeting or wayside encounter: the dart of a hare through a sheep creep in a stone wall, the flash of sunlight on the pavement after rain, jackdaws gathering to soak up the warmth from the rock, the sight of a solitary figure dropping down the terracing, fitful sunshine lighting up the rocks and disappearing, or the flash of a passing shadow.

For me these represent all that is best, expressing the quintessential excitement of this life-enriching place. Exploring its enigmas is what makes it special. It is a good place in which to spend time, on your own with your thoughts and dreams, or if you feel the need, in the company of others. I have come and gone, staying for days, weekends, and weeks on end. I have seen the small dramas of Burren life but have missed much more by not living here. But then, I ask myself, how could I miss it, if I lived here? Many people have visions of a secret home. It could be in the desert, the Canadian prairie, on top of mountains or in the bogs, under the sea, in the Bolivian wilderness, or in the Norwegian wasteland. The tourism PR and travel articles about the Burren sell it as a 'great wilderness', a 'moonscape' or 'lunar landscape', but these are tired phrases.

Whatever else it represents, the Burren is an experiment in time travel. What you find here depends on where you look and where you go. It is a rich cosmos, a place that reeks with a deep and enduring history and a charisma of its own. It has an endless capacity to surprise and inspire. When the wildlife writer Robert Macfarlane visited in 2005 with the naturalist Roger Deakin, he described it as a 'giant necropolis' and wrote about experiencing in a fort 'the swift deepening of time, the sharp sense of the preterite'.

There are manifold sides to it with disciplines of geography, geology, archaeology and botany leading the field. But the Burren, and what it represents, is more than the sum of the many ways in which it can be studied. Its spirit eludes some who come in search of it. Others return year after year to their favourite haunts, in favourite seasons, to their likes and dislikes, searching attentively in its innermost recesses. They have diverse interests, scientific and non-scientific, outdoors and indoors, underground and overground. But whatever their pursuits or their calling, they have one thing in common – an intention to find the spirit of the place and a desire to get drunk on the magic of the unique taste of their own personalised Burren wine. Burrenophilia is perhaps not as well known as Francophilia or Anglophilia but it is now a recognised, bona fide philia. Many have gained from the spirit of the Burren – not necessarily financial gain, but happiness, and for some a feeling of *inamorato*. The Burren requires time and inspires devotion in all who know it well. On my visits, I have followed one of the Dalai Lama's 18 Rules for Living: 'Once a year, go somewhere you have never been before.'

When Martha Gellhorn fell in love with the Rift Valley in East Africa she felt as if the quality of her blood had changed:

> Something new, rich and strong is pumping through my veins and exalting my heart, my lungs are filled with sunlit air, the world is too beautiful, I might easily spread my arms and fly.

Paragliding may be the nearest you could come to this state of mind, although I have never gone as far as jumping off the hills or trying to achieve parallel status with the fulmars or great black-backed gulls. But I have often felt the urgent and disturbing demand of the Burren in my bloodstream.

For several years in the 1990s local people, led by John D. MacNamara, organised an annual spring Burren Wildlife Symposium held in Ballinalacken Castle on the coast road near Doolin. They chose as their logo an image of the pine marten. This takes us back to the shy mustelid that slips sinuously and with a quiet secrecy across twilit roads. We have now a fair idea why it is particularly well adapted to life here and what it likes about the place. I cannot speak for *Martes martes*, but I reckon that we are in agreement in liking many of its special consolations: the potent allure of its emptiness, its roominess, its rawness, its uninhabitedness, its explorability, and its languid vastness. The theatre of nature appeals to us both. We have a joint hankering for open spaces and places to hide. I like the flowering of life in the spring, the way the sunlight spectacularly transmutes the rocks into ever-changing colours, and the constant play of light, through its shape-shifting shadows. I like the fact that it is a paean to the senses, a hymn to the pleasures of life and a place where you can taste nature at first hand. If you desire to know it, feel it, and live it, then walk its limestone, sample its silences and light, its uninterrupted horizons, and breathe the elixir of its air. Suffice to say that it exercises a power over you like nowhere else. It is an Arcadia, a place you feel at home in, after some acclimatising. Everything seems right with the world in this relaxing place. Once the Burren nirvana gets you in its vice-like grip, you are caught.

Each visit yields a rich harvest of memories with its own dynamic and makes me look at the world anew. After each sojourn within its ambit I realise what another Burren *habitué* Dr Charles Nelson meant when he wrote in his seminal companion to the wildflowers that the Burren is 'ineluctable'; there is no escape, once caught, forever smitten. Just one word sums it up. Like a disease, once experienced, it never lets you go. You are in its clutches. There is no cure. No visit to the doctor's, no amount of apples, pills or tablets, not even climbing a hazel tree (although I have tried it) will remedy this affliction. On each visit the days slip by all too quickly and still my *Itinerarium Curiousium* (Itinerary of Curiosities) continues to grow. The Burren can titillate too much. I wonder why two white horses have been chalked on a rock above the road near Poulawack, about the possible meaning of the Yggdrasil tree of life symbol on the Ó Lochlainn tomb at Corcomroe Abbey, about why the fox cub was acting suspiciously on the road at Ballyconry – these questions remain to be unlocked on other trips.

It is not possible to know a landscape exhaustively or comprehensively in all its disciplines. But each time I prepare to leave – my mind unsatiated – I point the car in the direction of home and the humdrum world of work that imprisons the spirit, I am loath to depart. A wistful and soft tristesse comes over me. I will return and in the interests of spiritual sustenance, breathe the limestone again, but part of my soul deep down remains here tied to a mystical compass point. To live here, I have concluded, would be a commitment that would eliminate the tickling of the surprise nodes that each return visit brings to somewhere that is irreplaceably and everlastingly itself.

Wedge Tomb, Poulaphuca © Marty Johnston

Coda

In 2009 the American guidebook publishers Frommer's brought out *500 Places to See Before They Disappear*, a list of the world's most endangered tourist destinations. Under the sub-heading 'One-of-a-kind Landscapes', the Burren was included (at No. 6) in the exalted company of the Columbia Icefields in Alberta, the Everglades in Southern Florida, the Pantanal wildlife zone in south-western Brazil, and the Purnululu National Park in Western Australia. The Burren was described as 'Ireland's stony wilderness . . . a fragile environment that is threatened by both too much and too little human attention'.

While there is no danger of the Burren disappearing in the foreseeable future, it is clear that it does receive a huge amount of attention. A glance at the bibliography that follows shows a proliferation of books about it in the past twenty years. In 1990, apart from some local guides and an academic flora, it was hard to find any detailed reference books to it. The publication in the early 1990s of Dr Charles Nelson's companion to the wildflowers, Gordon D'Arcy's natural history book, and the collection of essays in *The Book of the Burren* brought a heightened level of interest, opening the doors to a much wider audience.

Coda

Lest I have painted in this book too romantic a picture, everything in the clichéd Burren rock garden is not always rosy. It is often viewed, not so much through rose-tinted, but gentian-tinted, spectacles. There are enormous pressures from different quarters, and its heritage is under threat. Fortunately many highly committed and dedicated people are working to protect it.

Irish newspapers frequently carry stories about the alarming spread of scrub threatening the archaeological monuments and destroying the habitats of plants. This has been a worrying development in recent years and plans have been put in place to get the grazing balance right. In an effort to encourage visitors to help look after the landscape, the Burren Code was drawn up in 2000 promoting good practice for tourists. Signs in three languages were erected at busy locations urging visitors not to shatter large pieces of limestone or remove stones which were being indiscriminately taken from walls.

At the end of the first decade of the twenty-first century the Burren has a large number of people fighting its corner. It is now a much-labelled place with a heavy amount of acronymic armour-cladding and several organisations looking after its interests. Hard-working groups such as Burrenbeo, Burren Connect, Burren Way and the Burren Life Project, constantly highlight issues that need to be dealt with, and have done remarkable work in conservation and sustainability. Debates have been started and practical measures taken to help ensure the future of specific sites. Community and farming initiatives as well as campaigning by environmental groups have delivered benefits. Information, in the form of literature and on websites, is readily accessible through the Burrenbeo's education centre in Kinvara and at tourist information points in Ballyvaughan and Kilfenora.

But there are difficulties in funding and in raising awareness, and a holistic approach is lacking. No comprehensive landscape legislative framework is in place for Ireland. The protective labels themselves, while clearly important, will not secure the Burren's future. The government pumps money into helping it but still does not have a coherent integrated management plan for its future and appears unwilling to come up with any sort of properly structured long-term strategy.

In 2010 the Irish government selected the Burren as one of its tentative list of nominees to UNESCO as world heritage sites. The Office of Public Works announced that the Burren had taken over from Killarney National Park in being proposed as Ireland's prime natural landscape and that it had met the criteria of having Outstanding Universal Value (OUV). In the same year, a survey – carried out by an insurer of heritage buildings which asked people to name their favourite Irish heritage site – showed that the Burren came out on top and was the place most people would prefer to be granted UNESCO status.

The Burren is much-talked about. Conferences and colloquiums abound. There is much debate about conservation and even more conversation. Each May the Burren Law School, founded in 1994, precedes the Burren in Bloom festival when Ballyvaughan is animated with a curiosity and energy that few other places of a similar size can rival. Speakers from all over Ireland come to talk about the latest archaeological excavation, new thinking about orchids, or to throw some previously unknown light on turloughs.

At the annual Burren spring conference, held in early February and running since 1987, a staggering number of topics have been discussed, providing a wealth of illumination. The conference's mission statement is 'to provide a space where knowledge and ideas about the Burren may be shared, and practical actions undertaken to sustain this unique place, its communities and culture'.

Coda

On a visit in 2008, when he was speaking at the spring conference, Dr David Bellamy summed up the Burren succinctly calling it 'a time capsule of the last 6,000 years'. But he warned also that it is in danger of being loved too much. The challenge for the future is in sustaining the Burren and its communities while achieving the right balance and keeping the love for its OUV ever so slightly in check.

Mother and cub at Black Head © Marty Johnston

Glossary

Anthropomorphic Shaped like a human silhouette.

Bullaun stone A stone with a large, round, man-made depression.

Cairn Large mound of stones.

Capstone A large roofstone boulder covering the chamber of a megalithic tomb.

Cashel Fort made of stone, also known as a rath, ringfort or caher.

Chert A flint-like form of quartz found on limestone strata.

Cist Small box-like structure in which bodies were placed for burial.

Clints Horizontal slabs of limestone pavement.

Cromlech A nineteenth-century name for a dolmen.

Dolmen A chambered tomb supporting a capstone.

Fulacht fiadh An ancient cooking place.

Glacial erratics Large boulders carried by glacial action and deposited throughout the landscape.

Granite Hard igneous rock.

Grave goods Pottery and other offerings left in a tomb with the dead.

Grykes Deep, open fissures or crevices in the limestone pavement.

Kamenitza A shallow pool of limestone.

Karst An area formed by the weathering of soluble rocks and named after a region of Slovenia.

Limestone A sedimentary porous rock widespread throughout the Burren.

Megalithic Built from large stones, from the Greek *mega* (large) and *lithos* (stone).

Mesolithic Period between the early Stone Age and the late Stone Age.

Neolithic The late Stone Age, around 4000–2000 BC.

Polje A large enclosed valley or depression caused by erosion and surrounded by steep sides.

Rillenkarren Narrow, sharp-edged solution runnels formed on gently sloping limestone.

Souterrain An underground passage found in early medieval sites.

Stone circle A ring of spaced standing stones with a ritualistic purpose.

Turlough A lake that dries up in summer and is often filled with water in the winter.

Wedge tomb A megalithic tomb whose name is descriptive of its shape, tapering in height and width from front to back.

Burren Bibliography

Balfe, M., *A Burren Village*, Frenchman Publications, 2006
Brew, F., *Still Life: The glaciated valley of north Clare and south Galway*, 2004
Cunningham, G., *Burren Journey*, Shannonside, Limerick, 1978
— *Burren Journey West*, Shannonside Mid-Western, 1980
— *Burren Journey North*, Burren Research Press, 1992
— *Exploring the Burren*, Country House, 1998
Curtis, P. J., *The Music of Ghosts*, Old Forge Books, 2003
D'Arcy, G., *The Natural History of the Burren*, Immel, 1992
— *The Burren Wall*, Tír Eolas, 2006
Drew, D., *Burren Karst*, Geographical Association, 2001
Dunford, B., *Farming and the Burren*, Teagasc, 2002
Feehan, J., *The Secret Places of the Burren*, Carbery Books, 1987
Jones, C., *The Burren and the Aran Islands: Exploring the Archaeology*, The Collins Press, 2004
Karst Working Group (various eds), *The Karst of Ireland*, Geological Society of Ireland, 2000
Kirby, T., *The Burren & the Aran Islands: A Walking Guide*, The Collins Press, 2009
Krieger, C., *The Fertile Rock: Seasons in the Burren*, The Collins Press, 2006
Lysaght, L., *An Atlas of Breeding Birds of the Burren & Aran Islands*, BirdWatch Ireland, 2002
MacMahon, M., *On a Fertile Rock: The Cistercian Abbey of Corcomroe*, Kincora Books, 2000
Murphy, M. (ed.), *Máire Rua: Lady of Leamaneh*, Ballinakella Press, 1990
Nelson, C., *Wild Plants of the Burren and the Aran Islands*, The Collins Press, 1999
Nelson, C. & Walsh, W., *The Burren: A companion to the wildflowers of an Irish limestone wilderness*, Boethius Press & the Conservancy of the Burren, 1991
Ó Céirín, C., *The Outlandish World of the Burren*, Rathbane Publishing, 1998
O' Connell, J.W. & Korff, A. (eds), *The Book of the Burren*, Tír Eolas, 1991
O'Donohue, J., *Anam Cara*, HarperCollins, 1997
– *Conamara Blues*, Doubleday, 2000
Ó Laighléis, R., *Terror on the Burren*, Móinín, 1998
— *Battle for the Burren*, Móinín, 2007
Osborne, B. & Jones, M. (eds), *Understanding the Burren*, Royal Irish Academy, 2003
Owens, P., *Climbs in the Burren and Aran Islands*, Mountaineering Council of Ireland, 2008

Poyntz, S., *A Burren Journal,* Tír Eolas, 2000
— (ed.), *Burren Villages: Tales of History and Imagination,* Mercier Press, 2010
Praeger, R. L., *A Tourist's Flora of the West of Ireland,* Hodges, Figgis, 1909
— *The Way That I Went,* Hodges, Figgis, 1937
Robinson, T., *The Burren: a two-inch map of the uplands of north-west Clare,* Folding Landscapes, 1999
Self, C. A. (ed.), *Caves of County Clare,* University of Bristol Spelaeological Society, 1979
Simms, M., *Exploring the limestone landscapes of the Burren and the Gort lowlands,* Burrenkarst, 2001
Swinfen, A., *Forgotten Stones: Ancient church sites of the Burren and environs,* Lilliput Press, 1992
Tratman, E. K. (ed.), *Caves of North-West Clare, Ireland,* David & Charles.
Webb, D. A. & Scannell, M. J. P., *Flora of Connemara and the Burren,* Royal Dublin Society & Cambridge University Press, 1983
Westropp, T. J., *Archaeology of the Burren: Prehistoric Forts and Dolmens in North Clare,* Clasp Press, 1999 (reprint)

General Bibliography

Aalen, F. H. A. & Whelan, K., Stout, M. (eds), *Atlas of the Irish Rural Landscape,* Cork University Press, 1997
Abbey, E., *Desert Solitaire,* Ballantine Books, 1968
Bryson, B., *The Lost Continent,* Secker and Warburg, 1989
Bulfin, W., *Rambles in Eirinn,* M. H. Gill & Son, 1907
Bunbury, T., *The Irish Pub,* Thames & Hudson, 2008
Cabot, D., *The New Naturalist: Ireland,* HarperCollins, 1999
Cocker, M., *Crow Country,* Jonathan Cape, 2007
Cowie, D., *Ireland: The Land and the People,* A. S. Barnes, 1976
Curtis, P. J., *Notes from the Heart,* Poolbeg, 1994
Davies, D. W., *Megalith: Eleven Journeys in Search of Stones,* Gomer, 2006
Dunne, L. & Feehan, J., *Ireland's Mushroom Stones: Relics of a Vanished Lakeland,* University College Dublin, 2003
Fairley, J., *A Basket of Weasels,* James Fairley, 2001
Fanthorpe, U. A., *New & Collected Poems,* Enitharmon, 2010
Fitzgerald, M. A., *Thomas Johnson Westropp: An Irish Antiquary,* University College Dublin, 2000

General Bibliography

Gellhorn, M., *Travels with Myself and Another*, Allen Lane, 1978

Grigson, G., *Country Writings*, Century Publishing, 1984

Harbison, P., *Guide to National and Historic Monuments of Ireland*, Gill & Macmillan, 1992

Harding, J. M., *Discovering Irish Butterflies & their Habitats*, 2008

Hayward, R., *Munster and the City of Cork*, Phoenix, 1964

Heaney, S., *The Spirit Level*, Faber, 1996

Hughes, H., *Frommer's 500 Places to See Before They Disappear: A Celebration of the World's Fragile Wonders*, Frommer, 2009

Jennett, S., *Munster*, Faber, 1967

Kohn, M., *Turned Out Nice*, Faber, 2010

Longley, M., *Collected Poems*, Cape Poetry, 2006

Mabey, R., *Selected Writings, 1974–1999*, Chatto & Windus, 1999

— *Nature Cure*, Chatto & Windus, 2005

McCaig, E. (ed.), *The Poems of Norman MacCaig*, Polygon, 2009

McConnell, B. (ed.), *Geology of Galway Bay*, Geological Survey of Ireland, 2004

McDonald, B. (ed.), *Extreme Landscape: The Lure of Mountain Spaces*, National Geographic Society, 2002

Macfarlane, R., *Mountains of the Mind*, Granta, 2003

— *The Wild Places*, Granta, 2007

Mac Liammóir, M., *Ireland*, Thames & Hudson, 1966

MacNeice, L., *Collected Poems 1925–1948*, Faber, 1949

Mills, S., *Nature in its Place: The Habitats of Ireland*, Bodley Head, 1987

Neillands, R., *Walking Through Ireland*, Little, Brown & Company, 1993

Newby, E., *Round Ireland in Low Gear*, Collins, 1987

O'Brien, K., *My Ireland*, Batsford, 1962

Perrin, J., *West: A Journey through the Landscapes of Loss*, Atlantic Books, 2010

Pilcher, J. & Hall, V., *Flora Hibernica*, The Collins Press, 2001

Rackard, A., *Fish Stone Water: The Holy Wells of Ireland*, Attic Press, 2000

Robinson, T., *Setting Foot on the Shores of Connemara & Other Writings*, Lilliput Press, 1996

— *Connemara: Listening to the Wind*, Penguin, 2006

Somerville-Large, P., *The Grand Irish Tour*, Hamish Hamilton, 1982

Thackeray, W., *The Irish Sketchbook, 1842*, Blackstaff Press, 1985

Twohig, E.S., *Irish Megalithic Tombs*, Shire Publications, 2004

Viney, M., *Ireland: A Smithsonian Natural History*, Blackstaff Press, 2003

Wallis, C., *Richard Long: Heaven and Earth*, Tate Publishing, 2009

Acknowledgements

This book has been written for the pleasure of thinking about the Burren, going there to gather the material and talking to those who know it well. In the writing of it I have received help and inspiration from many people. First of all, I would like to thank Dr Ralph Forbes who prised open the Burren wildflower door many years ago on a memorable spring field trip organised through Queen's University, Belfast.

My agent Jonathan Williams provided unending support and steered *Burren Country* to its destination. I am grateful to Gordon and Esther-Mary D'Arcy for reading and commenting on the manuscript, spotting some scientific solecisms and suggesting improvements. They also shared their deep well of Burren knowledge and offered me hospitality at their home. I would like to thank Margaret Ó Loclainn (not least for the welcoming nips of whiskey), Sarah Poyntz, Fr. Des Forde, Ré Ó Laighléis, Seán Tyrrell and Manus Walsh for agreeing to be interviewed at length, for their patience in answering all my questions and giving unstintingly of their time.

Three writers, Mary O'Malley, Michael Fewer and Tony Kirby, provided fruitful discussion and guidance during Burren rambles. Valuable local information as well as titbits of gossip came from Madeleine Quinn, Jim McCarthy, Jim Hyland and the staff of the Hyland's Burren Hotel.

Michael Williams of NUI Galway kindly helped me locate and put in context the glacial erratics. On several occasions Seán Fagan identified wild flowers previously known to me only through photographs in books of flora and I thank him and Frances Chapman. Sharon Parr and Stephen Ward imparted their knowledge of matters Burren through guided talks.

It has been a pleasure to walk the limestone pavement in the company of two former BBC colleagues, both now master photographers, Marty Johnston and Trevor Ferris whose artistic work considerably enhances this book and who were exceptionally generous in supplying photographs as well as giving of their time. Marty

Acknowledgements

provided the perfect muse with his cover photograph and offered many imaginative suggestions. For his graphic design skills, I am particularly indebted to Colin McCadden who drew the map I had in mind.

I wish to thank Joe Bruton for allowing me to stay in his cottage in Berneens in the heart of the Burren; I cannot think of a more stimulating and idyllic location in which to write. Nick Condon of Shannon Development has helped me with several Burren-related projects and I thank him for his assistance.

I am most grateful to all those who, since 2008, have actively supported my spring creative writing workshops in Ballyvaughan. The chorus of writers from the Whiterock (appropriate in a Burren context) class run by Belfast Metropolitan College deserve particular mention for their friendship and sense of adventure in coming with me, and I salute them all: Fionnuala Burke, Denis Carson, Kevin Cassidy, Martin Devlin, Marie Forrester, Tom Hannon, George Magennis, Mary Molloy, Christopher Owens, John Robinson, Lila and Phil Stuart, and Bobby Walsh. Thanks are also due to Geraldine Burke, Catherine Byrne, Emma Caffrey, Olive Campbell, Fionnuala Collins, Bernard Conlon, Leo and Margaret Convery, Margaret Costello, Orla Cunningham, Fiona Ellis-Chadwick, Noreen Erskine, Phyl Foley, Lynda Foy, Liz Gough, Anne Hailes, David Harland, Christine Healy, Colette Healy, Declan Henry, Catherine Keating, Patricia Kernaghan, Jonathan Martin, Hugh McCaw, Elaine McComb, Jean McConaghy, Hilary Murnane, Mary O'Sullivan, Julia Paul, Melissa Poiset, Brian Searle, Liz Shaw, John Simpson, Evelyn Smyth, Sarah Thorn, and Colette Walker.

Several of the essays, in slightly different and shorter form, originally appeared in *The Irish Times*, the *Guardian, Ireland of the Welcomes, Escape*, and *The Clare Champion* and I thank the editors of these publications. Warm thanks to David Torrans at No Alibis Bookshop in Belfast who has supported my previous books and who introduced me several years ago to the work of Edward Abbey, otherwise known as 'Cactus Ed'.

I gratefully acknowledge all those authors and poets from whose books I have quoted extracts. Michael Longley kindly agreed to allow as a preliminary the use of his poem 'Burren Prayer', published by

Jonathan Cape in *Collected Poems*, 2006. 'The Burren' is from U. A. Fanthorpe's *New & Collected Poems*, published by Enitharmon Press, 2010. The extract from 'A Burren Prayer', from *Conamara Blues* by John O'Donohue and published by Doubleday, is reprinted by permission of the Random House Group Ltd. 'Sligo and Mayo' is extracted from the 'The Closing Album' published by Faber in *Collected Poems, 1925– 1948* by Louis MacNeice and is reprinted by permission of David Higham Associates Ltd. The extract from 'Thirst in the Burren' by Moya Cannon is from *Carrying the Songs*, published in 2007, and is reprinted by permission of Carcanet Press Ltd. Every effort has been made to contact copyright holders. Any omissions will be rectified at the earliest opportunity.

If I have inadvertently left out any names, I apologise and offer a heartfelt thank you to everyone. My greatest thanks go to my wife Felicity and son Daniel (who first glimpsed the Burren's limestone pavement aged four months). They have provided a bedrock of support and ceaseless encouragement for my projects undertaken a long way from home. I dedicate this book jointly to them, as well as to all Burren travellers.

Paul Clements,
Belfast, January 2011

Websites

www.ballyvaughanireland.com
www.burrenbeo.com
www.burrencollege.ie
www.burrenconnect.ie
www.burrenforts.ie
www.burrenlife.com
www.burrennationalpark.ie
www.burrentolkiensociety.ie
www.masterphotographers.co.uk
www.PhotoLanna.com
www.theburrencentre.ie

Index

Index